BE FREE

BE FREE

FINDING FULLNESS OF LIFE WITH GOD

ERIK SWENSON

INDEPENDENT PUBLISHER

Copyright © 2018 by Erik Swenson. All rights reserved. Applies to text, illustrations, and photographs.

Published by IM PRESS
A division of Incarnate Ministries
www.incarnateministries.com

All rights reserved. No part of this publication may be reproduced by any means—for example, electronic, photocopy, recording—without prior written permission of the publisher.

ISBN 10: 0-6928-8982-5
ISBN 978-0-6928-8982-4

Scripture quotations are from the New Revised Standard Version Bible, copyright © 1989 the Division of Christian Education of the National Council of the Churches of Christ in the United States of America. Used by permission. All rights reserved.

Because of the dynamic nature of the Internet, any web addresses or links contained in this book may have changed since publication.

*For Heather:
Apart from Jesus Christ, you are the most
truthful person I know.*

CONTENTS

Introduction: The Promise Is Freedom But ...

1) Do What You Want: *Why We Chose Independence*

2) Bobbing in the Middle of an Ocean: *Imprisoned by Sin*

3) Bad Dads: *Changing Our Picture of God*

4) The Lion Who Became a Lamb: *How Jesus Sets Us Free*

5) Giving the Eulogy at My Own Funeral: *Dying in Order to Live*

6) A Water Bottle for Astronauts: *Escaping Condemnation*

7) Made Out of Plastic: *Overcoming Temptation*

8) Taller Than a Tower: *Conquering Fear*

9) The Man Who Bought a Field: *Opening Up to God*

10) Sitting on a Song: *Being Filled by the Spirit*

11) A Body That Can't Be Killed: *Love Leads Us into Freedom*

12) Not as Free as I'm Gonna Be: *Progress vs. Perfection*

Appendices

Acknowledgments

Notes

AUTHOR'S NOTE

This is a book about finding freedom from sin so we can experience the fullness of life that is available with God. One thing that qualifies me to write a book about sin is that I've done it a lot. Notice I refer to my sins as things I've done rather than something I am. More on this to come, but for now, I can simply say that I've learned my past sin does not define me—God's love does.

I should also say that this book isn't filled with theory. For the last five years I've been on a mission to understand freedom because I desperately need it. What follows is the result of everything I've learned and continue to apply. I hope the knowledge within will help you as much as it has helped me. I still have a long way to go, but I'm not who I used to be.

Because of the work of Jesus, freedom is available to all of us. Progress is possible. We really can be free. Now I want to share with you how.

INTRODUCTION

THE PROMISE IS FREEDOM BUT...

THE PROBLEM OF SIN

I don't know when I became a Christian. My earliest memory is sitting in a laundry basket with my cousin. I'm not sure how old we were but we were small enough to both fit in a laundry basket. The reason I remember this is because he leaned over and bit me on the arm, without any provocation. Everything is blurry after that because I started crying. But as far as I know, I didn't retaliate. I like to tell people that since I turned the other cheek I must have been converted sometime before this incident.

But the truth is, I didn't continue to turn the other cheek. In fact, a few years later, I was in our garage arguing with the neighbor kid and I bit him on the arm. It stopped the argument but also landed me in the corner for hours (which was a just sentence).

It didn't take long for me to realize I had a problem and that I'm not alone. Just turn on the news and you will find people biting each other all over the place. Something is clearly wrong with our world. The Bible identifies our problem as sin and it is common to all humanity. The Apostle Paul said, "all have sinned and fall short of the glory of God" (Romans 3:23).

But what is sin? Most of us hear the word and think of specific examples. It can be helpful to cite examples, but we need a definition so we can identify what we are up against. The Greek word for sin is *hamartia* and it simply means "missing the mark." We were created in the beginning to receive our life from God and to live in relationship with God—that is our mark. In the book of Acts, it says that in God we "live and move and have our being" (17:28). And Jesus taught us that the greatest commandment, and therefore our greatest purpose, is to love God and love each other (Luke 10:27).

But Satan deceived humanity into believing that we could find life and fulfillment apart from God (Genesis 3). He prompted us to aim for something other than God. So, we chose to run away, thereby breaking the relationship. Humanity cut itself off from the life source, and death entered our story. The world has been dying ever since. We can all feel this death pressing in, and it sends us into survival mode. In desperation, we grasp for anything we can find to bring some fulfillment or at least some relief. Not all the things we reach for are inherently bad, but they were never intended to ultimately sustain us. We may feel alive for a time, but it doesn't last. So, we keep going back for more and we eventually become addicted and imprisoned. We become trapped because of sin.

Sin also impacts our relationships. In our search for life, we are often willing to fight others, use others, or, at the very least, neglect others to find what we are looking for. Sin destroys our ability to love and it leads us to relational brokenness. In addition to all of the issues caused by our own sin, we also carry deep brokenness from the sins committed against us. This brokenness helps galvanize the bars to our prison.

Jesus said that anyone who sins is a slave to sin (John 8:34). The author of Proverbs said that our iniquities ensnare us (5:22). And in the second letter to Timothy, we learn about our need to escape from the snare of the devil, the one holding people captive (2:26). This imprisonment ultimately leads to death. Paul wrote, "the wages of sin is death" (Romans 6:23).

As bleak as all this sounds, there is hope, for the Bible also offers a promise of liberation from our bondage. Jesus identified freedom as the purpose of his mission. He said he came to free the oppressed and imprisoned and to bind up the brokenhearted (Luke 4:18; Isaiah 61:1). His friend John explained that Jesus came to destroy the works of the devil (1 John 3:8). The Bible also says that Jesus abolished death (2 Timothy 1:10). He came to make a way back to God, and he calls us to follow him into freedom.

That is the promise—freedom from sin, from Satan, and from death. Jesus said that if the "Son makes you free, you will be free indeed" (John 8:36). Paul said we have "been set free from sin" (Romans 6:18).

THE PROMISE IS FREEDOM BUT...

The work has already been accomplished and now we can learn to live in this new reality.

This is great news, but it presented me with a problem. The promise is freedom, but I didn't feel free. My experience said something else. The freedom felt false. I consistently felt like a prisoner to sin, and I kept doing things I didn't want to do. I kept looking for life—apart from God—and living in the rhythm of falling, then repenting. This pattern defined my reality. It felt like running on an inclined treadmill and never reaching the destination. I thought I was hopeless and assumed God only tolerated me.

I believe not feeling the freedom that Christ promises is common to many Jesus followers, and it leads to two questions:

1) Why don't we experience the freedom that Jesus promised?
2) What must we do to live free?

The good news is, I've found the answers to both of these questions.

WHY DON'T WE EXPERIENCE FREEDOM?

If it is true that Jesus has set us free, why doesn't our experience confirm this? How is it possible we are actually free when we still feel like we are in prison? The answer is simple . . . we believe lies. You see, it is possible to remain in prison even if the cell door is unlocked.

Years ago, I was talking to my friend Morgan. I was telling my story and mostly lamenting about my failures. When I finished, Morgan described the picture that came to his mind when he was listening to me. He saw me curled up on the ground in a jail cell. It was a damp place, the kind of prison where they slide your food on a metal plate through a slot in the door. Then his mental camera panned out, revealing that the door to my prison cell wasn't locked. Morgan looked at me and said, "You don't have to stay there."

BE FREE

I was leveled by this revelation. I knew the prison well—the way you know the home you grew up in. It never occurred to me that I could just walk out. So, for years I'd just been sitting there, huddled in the corner.

The truth is Jesus kicked open the door. He came and liberated us. We don't have to stay in prison anymore. Not only has Jesus unlocked the door but he also calls us to follow him into freedom. But he does not force us to leave. We have a choice, which means we can choose to stay put. But why would anyone want to stay in prison? I believe there are at least two reasons.

First, it is possible for us to be in denial. When you've been locked up a long time, you may not see it as a prison anymore. Things may not be great, but the walls become familiar. We get comfortable with our situation. We can become so used to our sin that we don't see it as sin any longer. Jesus was once talking to some people about how sin leads us into slavery and they responded by saying, "We are descendants of Abraham and have never been slaves to anyone" (John 8:33). They were blind to their condition.

If this happens, we may not really see a need to leave. Brooks was a character in the movie *The Shawshank Redemption*. He had been an inmate most of his life and when they released him, he was an old man. Brooks got a job bagging groceries, and even though he was a free man, he still asked the manager permission to use the bathroom. He couldn't get the prison out of his head. Sometimes he even

THE PROMISE IS FREEDOM BUT...

thought about committing another crime so they would send him back. He had been "institutionalized" and so have many of us.

The other reason we may choose to stay in prison is because we become filled with despair. Some of us are aware of the prison and desperately want to get out but eventually we just lose hope of finding freedom. We may believe that because of our sin God is indifferent toward us, or perhaps he is angry with us. Many of us believe God has chosen to leave us to sleep in the bed we made. It is possible to be so discouraged we simply never look up from the floor to realize there is a way out. This was my story. It took a friend looking at my life from the outside to point out that the door was open.

Both denial and despair are based in deception. If I don't believe I'm in an actual prison, I am deceived. But if I don't believe I can experience freedom from this prison, I am also deceived. God did not abandon us in our sin, nor is it his aim to punish us. Instead he came to liberate and restore us. Freedom is real and it is available. It is possible for things to change. This leads us to the second question . . .

WHAT CAN WE DO TO LIVE FREE?

We've stayed in prison because of deception and the way to overcome deception is with truth. Here is the way that Jesus explained it. "If you continue in my word, you are truly my disciples; and you will know the truth, and the truth will make you free" (John 8:31–32).

Most often we focus on the second part of Jesus' statement—if we know the truth, it will make us free. And this is a good starting point. We do need to know the truth to find freedom. The Greek word for truth is *aletheia*, which means "reality unveiled," or more literally, "not covered." To know truth is to uncover reality and to align our minds with it. Paul said we can be transformed by the renewing of our minds (Romans 12:2). We need to take ownership and know that sin is real and it keeps us in prison. And we also need to know that Jesus destroyed the power of sin to set us free because he loves us. His love has the power to restore us. This knowledge will help us begin to pick apart the lies of Satan that seek to keep us in prison. As Paul wrote, we can "stand against the wiles of the devil" (Ephesians 6:11). While this is vital, there is more to this process. We need more than just head knowledge.

Jesus said we will know the truth that frees us if we hold to his teaching and thus become his disciples. The thing that leads to truth—and therefore, freedom—is becoming a disciple. What does it mean to become a disciple? A disciple is one who is disciplined by another. It is one who comes under the direction and lordship of another who is greater. To be a disciple, one must respond to an invitation to follow. When Jesus called Peter and the others to follow him, they "brought their boats to shore, they left everything and followed him" (Luke 5:11). These men became not only his disciples but his friends. They lived in close relationship with Jesus. His love changed them and they became filled with his life and his power.

Jesus said the truth sets us free, but he also said he is the truth (John 14:6). He even used the same word *aletheia*. So, to say the truth sets us free is to say that Jesus sets us free. He is the reality of God unveiled, and we need him. We don't just need the right ideas, we need Jesus. It is choosing to live in relationship with him that frees us. This is not a passive exercise. Action is required. The disciples chose to get out of the boat and followed him. In the same way, we can and must choose to step out of prison and walk with Jesus.

SOME CLARIFICATION

I want to pause here because I've just raised at least a few concepts that warrant further explanation.

First, I provided a definition of sin that is rather all encompassing. Instead of thinking about sin as the "bad" stuff that we should avoid, I am suggesting that we sin anytime we try to find life and fulfillment apart from God—or anytime we walk outside of God's will for us. Some may hear this and think I'm being zealous and making a big deal out of nothing. I realize this definition may be somewhat overwhelming.

THE PROMISE IS FREEDOM BUT...

You may be saying, I knew I struggled with these three things, but now I have ten more to add to the list. But let me put you at ease. Our search for independence is what took us into prison. The solution is not to focus on stopping bad behaviors, which usually doesn't work. The solution is to return to a dependence on God so we can be filled with his life again. That is a good trade.

Second, in saying that we need to make a choice to step out of prison and walk with Jesus, I am suggesting that we need to do something to experience our freedom. This may sound like I am saying we are responsible or that we deserve credit for our freedom. This is not the case. We could never free ourselves, nor would we want to, without God's intervention. Paul said that the sinful mind is "hostile" toward God (Romans 8:7). In our sin we counted God an enemy. Jesus did the work of liberating us—period. Through his life, death, resurrection, and ascension, he blasted open the door and made the way. He is the one rousing us from sleep, to wake us up to the possibility of freedom. But he does not force us to leave. In setting us free, he restored our choice. Paul said that Jesus removed the veil that hardened our minds (2 Corinthians 3:14). It is only through the power of Jesus' work and the influence of the Holy Spirit that we are able to choose, but you and I still must exercise that choice and respond. This is a good thing because it means we are not passive victims. We can do something about our situation. We can vacate the musty prison cell and never look back.

If we don't step out, we will remain in prison. And if we don't walk with Jesus, we will end up trying to walk alone and will inevitably end up back in prison. Why? It was our independence that landed us in prison in the first place.

Third, you may be wondering how it is possible to have a relationship with Jesus when he is not here with us in the flesh any longer. Once I was driving in the mountains and I saw a figure standing in the middle of a field. I pulled over to investigate and discovered it was a statue of Jesus propped up on a pile of rocks. Sometimes I think it would be nice to be able to find Jesus in a field and go talk with him in person. I mean, how do you relate to an invisible man?

BE FREE

But here is the thing: Jesus did not leave us alone when he returned to the Father (John 14:18–25). He gave us the Holy Spirit, who makes it possible for us to have a tangible relationship with God. Notice I said "who" when referring to the Holy Spirit. The reason is because we often think God's Spirit is an impersonal force like fire or wind or electricity. These powerful forces accomplish things, but they aren't very relational. But the Holy Spirit has a personality and is a member of the Trinity just like the Father and the Son. We will go into greater depth on this vital relationship throughout the book. For now, it's worth noting that God still wants to speak to us. This is one role of the Holy Spirit. I will explain this process more in Chapter 10 but throughout the book, I will make references to the internal voice of the Holy Spirit offering revelation and direction. By revelation, I mean an increased understanding of God's word and character.

Finally, I've stated that this is a simple process. Simple and easy are not the same thing. This journey will likely feel hard at times. It will feel hard because the problem runs deep. We have given ourselves over to many things in our search for life. A. W. Tozer refers to these as the "tough, fibrous roots" of the heart.[1] We must be willing to allow these things to be uprooted so we can experience the life and freedom God has for us.

Sometimes we don't like to hear about hard. We prefer easy . . . I know I do. Many of us spend a great deal of time trying to make life more comfortable, and we search for the path of least resistance. But the truth is, making the jail cell cozier will not lead us into freedom. The difficulties we will encounter can't begin to compare with the life and freedom that Jesus offers us.

THE ROAD AHEAD

Before we go further, I want to provide an overview for where we are headed.

1) **Stepping Out:** I've mentioned that the first step in finding freedom is to stand up and step out of the prison. This process begins with a choice. However, before we are able to really make that choice, we need to have a strong grasp on the seriousness of our problem. We need to see what got us into prison and what has kept us there. Then we need to understand the solution that God has made available. Through an act of love that is almost beyond our comprehension, Jesus took actions to destroy the power of sin, Satan, and death (see Appendix A). Despite what we may think, he is not angry or indifferent toward us. He intervened to save us and this freedom is available to all who want it. When we come to terms with our sin and with God's response to it, we are ready to make the decision to abandon our independence and entrust our lives to Jesus.

2) **Walking with God:** This process is not a one-time decision. Freedom begins with the decision to walk out, but Jesus wants us to stay free. He wants to rehabilitate us so we never go back. This involves entering into a relationship with God. The relationship is the source of our freedom. Satan opposes our relationship with God and will try to condemn, tempt, and intimidate to keep us from freedom. The first step is to expose the deception and then demonstrate how we can overcome with God. With all of this in place, we will look at the very practical and tangible tools available to us to build a relationship with God through the Holy Spirit. It is through this process that we will truly begin to experience the freedom and fullness of life available to us. While we are going to walk through a process of individual transformation, it is impossible to separate it from our relationships. Sin gives us a chronic inward focus that hinders us from loving others, which is the whole reason we are here and the purpose for our freedom. As we begin to experience freedom in Christ, we are able to love others

more fully, and this gives way to a beautiful paradox. Because the more we practice love, the less we will be preoccupied with ourselves, which will lead to greater freedom.

Remember, this is a process and, thus, the goal is progress. We are already free, but we are also learning to be free.

ADDITIONAL RESOURCES

Our problem and our solution are simple. The path to freedom involves replacing lies with truth and walking in relationship with Jesus, who is the truth. I fully believe this and it is the main point of this book. Having said that, I need to acknowledge there are certain complexities to be aware of.

First, we will be dealing with the mind. The mind is strange. It is not a material thing, but it is inextricably attached to the brain, which is a physical organ. Chemical imbalances and/or injury to the brain can impact the mind and vice versa.

Next, we are all vastly unique, and so various struggles and addictions impact us in different ways. Alcohol, for example, seems to be highly addictive for some, but for others it is easy to consume in moderation.

Finally, while we are responsible for our own choices, and therefore, our own sins, we are also greatly impacted by the choices and sins of others. Some of the bondage we feel to certain sins can be directly related to things that happened to us.

This book is meant to be an overarching approach to finding freedom. If any of these complexities feel relevant to your story, this book will still help you, but you may also want to go deeper in a certain area. With this in mind, I've included a resource list at the end of the book (see Appendix B). I strongly recommend these materials as you pursue freedom.

CHAPTER 1

DO WHAT YOU WANT
WHY WE CHOSE INDEPENDENCE

DEFINING FREEDOM

We used to have a bunch of pet fish. Then all but one died. We moved this last fish from the tank to a small bowl containing one plastic plant and a few rocks. The fish did fine for a while. Then he started to move around less. His fins became tattered and his body started to look transparent, like a ghost fish. He stayed by the rocks all the time. When he would try to swim, he just spun in circles.

One night we decided to let the fish go. I grabbed the bowl, and my wife gathered our kids. We walked down to the pond behind our house to transfer him to the water. Then my daughter began to cry. She cried in deep sobs that shook her small shoulders. Her nose ran and mixed with tears, her face glistened. Heather tried to calm her as I picked her up. Ellie explained through cries that she was going to miss the fish. I tried to convince her the fish would be much happier in the large pond. Then I told her we could be glad because now the fish was free.

Once she realized our intent was to help him, she seemed to calm down. Plus, I offered to give her some string cheese.

This story provides a simple metaphor for prison and, more importantly, freedom. To be imprisoned is to be held against your will. The holding cell, whether it is a glass bowl or a set of chains, always leads to the slow, steady deterioration of the prisoner. Think of the half-dead fish drifting in circles.

Freedom is the opposite. To be set free is to get out of prison. The chains are smashed apart, the jail walls fall down, and the ex-con steps out into the open air. It is true that becoming free means to escape from prison or bondage. But we can take the definition of freedom

BE FREE

too far by saying freedom means a rejection of all authority. There is a tendency to equate freedom with complete independence.

We want to be in charge of our own lives and to exercise our unbridled will. As the poet William Ernest Henley wrote, "I am the master of my fate / I am the captain of my soul." I recently came across a journal of mine from fourth grade. In response to the question, "What does freedom mean to you?" I wrote, "To me freedom means being able to do what you want."

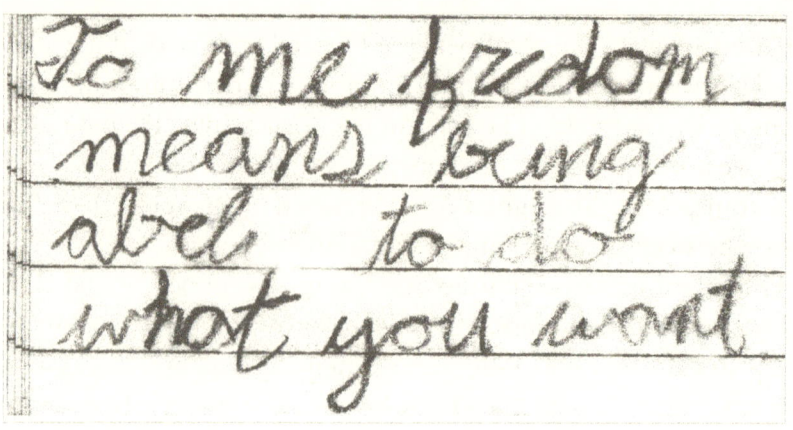

It is not just poets and young boys who think this way. This idea hangs heavily in our cultural atmosphere. America is the land of the free and we produce ideas like:

"Be the boss of you." —National Car Rental

"Have it your way," now changed to "Be your way." —Burger King

"Rule yourself." —Under Armour

The pursuit of fierce independence and getting what we want is one of the predominant values of our culture. This is the reason so many refer to marriage as the "old ball and chain." The idea that we may have to submit or compromise or consider another's will before our own is often equated with prison. There is a temptation to resist anything that may prevent us from doing what we want. People didn't always think this way, though. Our drive for independence is something we acquired.

IN THE BEGINNING

Genesis contains a beautiful story explaining the inception of humanity. The writer describes a God who made a definitive choice to create, and who delighted in what he made. God spoke, and most of the physical world materialized. He made things with his words. When God created humanity, he moved even closer. He picked up clay from the ground and formed it into a person. It says that Adam was made from dust and then God breathed his life into him and filled Adam with his Spirit. Adam became the collision point between earth and heaven—made from dirt but filled with the wind of God (Genesis 2:7).

After man was created, God said it was not good for him to be alone. So God put the man to sleep and took a bone from his body to create a woman (Genesis 2:18–22). This woman was tangible. The man could see her and touch her and she could relate to him in the same way. And they both carried the image of God (Genesis 1:27).

Some read the creation story literally and others suggest the author was using poetry to explain a profound truth about our origin. Either way, a deep reality is being conveyed—God is both the giver and sustainer of life. Adam and Eve were dependent on him to stay alive. God even gave them food, and he caused a stream to come up from the ground to water the garden (Genesis 1:29, 2:6).

Though they were dependent on him, they were not prisoners. They lived in relationship with God. This relationship was meant to last forever. The Biblical concept of relationship was a covenant in which the two parties bound themselves together for life. And when God makes a covenant, he does not break it (Deuteronomy 7:9, 31:8).

As a part of the covenant, God also gave the people responsibility. He delegated authority to them. God invited the man to name the animals (Genesis 2:19) and both man and woman were entrusted to

BE FREE

care for and defend creation (Genesis 1:26–29). By entrusting people with this responsibility, God was not treating them as servants but as friends (John 15:15).

But even more amazing than the shared authority, God also gave them freedom—specifically the freedom to decide. The surest evidence of their freedom was a tree that God placed in the middle of the garden. God said they could eat from every other tree but instructed them to stay away from the tree of the knowledge of good and evil (Genesis 2:16–17). Though God issued restrictions around the tree, he did not wrap the perimeter with a fence or rig it with explosives. The first people were at liberty to touch the tree and eat from it, though it was not God's will for them to do so. As pastor and author Bruxy Cavey points out, it was a "place of choice." God made them decision-makers, which means he intended them to be free.

But why? If God possesses all power, he could have kept people under control. Why give us freedom? The answer is love. The aim of every healthy relationship is that love can be given and returned. This is true for parents and children, and it is true for marriage. Love seeks the good of the other. If one party in the relationship is only a controlling consumer, the system doesn't work. You can't have a real relationship without love and you can't have love without freedom. It must be chosen.

Power can be used to gain almost anything in the world. If you have an army or guns or money or authority, you can force people to give you what you want. But love is the one exception. Love cannot be coerced. An effort to mandate love from someone can generate the opposite reaction in them.

In the movie *Gladiator*, the oppressive emperor enslaves his own sister and nephew. He cultivates a twisted, sensual love for the woman and plans to force her into marriage. Near the end of the film, there is a scene where he is circling around her like a dragon as she seems to stare through him. Her face is white except for shadows under her eyes where her tears have carved out two valleys. He tells the women she must not only marry him, but she must love him. He suggests to her that this command is an act of mercy because he has chosen to spare her life. When she doesn't respond, the emperor grabs her by the jaw and lurches toward her. With his hot breath on her face, he screams, "Am I not merciful?" It only solidifies her hatred.

God allows us to be free so genuine love is possible. He wants us to be able to reciprocate his love and to love each other. Jesus would later confirm these as the two greatest commandments (Matthew 22:36–40). Love is the whole point.

Unfortunately, there is an inherent risk in doing this. If love can be freely given it can also be withheld. If the first couple were free to stay, they were also free to leave. And this is what happened. It happened to them and it happens to all of us.

Humanity started in a good place—walking in the garden of God. But Adam and Eve made a decision to veer away from God. This change was prompted by what might seem like a harmless conversation between the couple and a crafty character called the serpent (Genesis 3:1). But as we know, it was not harmless.

This ancient serpent would later be identified as the devil (or Satan), who is the deceiver of the whole world (Revelation 12:9). Jesus confirmed this when he called Satan the father of lies. Interestingly, in the same breath, Jesus also said that the devil was a murderer from the beginning (John 8:44). He made a connection between Satan's deception and a violent desire to bring harm. The crafty serpent was not just trying to trick Adam and Eve, he was trying to kill them.

BE FREE

So how did he do this? By trying to lead them away from God. Author Dallas Willard wrote, "[Satan] did not hit [them] with a stick, but with an idea."[1] The idea was independence. Satan promised freedom through independence.

CHOOSING INDEPENDENCE

When the serpent came to talk with Eve, he spoke about God like God was not there. He started, "Did God really say . . ." As Bruxy Cavey explains, the serpent introduced the idea that it was possible to exist apart from God, which was something Adam and Eve hadn't considered. The Deceiver went on to explain why it was not only possible, but desirable. He said if they ate from the tree, they would become like God (Genesis 3:5). In other words, they could be their own gods.

This enemy spoke like one with experience. He already possessed the knowledge he was offering to Eve. It was not just an invitation to leave God, but to follow him to a place without God. Because the truth is, he had once lived in the presence of God, too, but he chose to reject his maker to become a god unto himself (Isaiah 14:12–14).

He spoke like a poet and said they could be masters of their own fate. And they believed him. The garden began to look like a prison meant to isolate us rather than a sanctuary meant to protect. Eve saw what the serpent was offering and it looked life-giving. So she took it. By doing so, she declared her independence from God. Then the woman gave some to the man who was with her. He ate too (Genesis 3:6). Recognize the man was standing there the whole time. He was equally responsible.

It sounds like a simple choice, but it set humanity on a course that would seem impossible to recover from. Even a subtle shift can alter the trajectory of an object. In the C. S. Lewis classic *The Screwtape Letters*, the fallen angel, Screwtape, describes this process by saying:

> We know that we have introduced a change of direction in his course which is already carrying him out of

> his orbit around [God] . . . He must not be allowed to suspect that he is now, however slowly, heading right away from the sun on a line which will carry him into the cold and dark of utmost space.[2]

Satan's voice was like a spark that ignited the fuel and humanity was set on a course that led away from God out into empty space. They thought they were choosing freedom, but quickly discovered the freedom they had been promised was a lie. It didn't feel like freedom. It was more like isolation.

For the first time, the people felt fear and shame. Accusation became a part of their conversation. The ground gave birth to thistles and physical pain became a harsh reality. Within the first generation, men were killing one another. The life they hoped to find apart from God was a myth. Instead, they found only death (Genesis 3–4).

Adam and Eve's decision to eat from the tree of the knowledge of good and evil is often referred to as the original sin. Remember the word for "sin" is *hamartia*, which means to "miss the mark." The people were dependent on God. He kept them alive. But they rejected God to pursue their independence. They went the wrong direction and ended up in a place without him. They cut themselves off from the Life-giver and thus forfeited their lives. The covenant was broken.

Imagine you are in a hospital bed hooked up to a breathing machine, and you are also receiving medication through an IV. The breathing tubes and drugs are keeping you alive. Then someone comes into the room and tells you they have something that will help you recover more quickly, but you have to follow them to another floor of the hospital. Unfortunately, the offer is a lie. If you make the decision to pull out the IV and disconnect the oxygen tube so you can leave your bed, you will not survive very long.

Death was not an imposed or judicial punishment; it was an intrinsic one that flowed naturally out of a decision to reject God. Death is what happens in the absence of life, and it is something we chose. This is why Paul said the wages of sin is death (Romans 6:23).

BE FREE

This is not just an ancient Biblical story—it is our story. Ever person who has ever lived has made the decision to pursue life apart from God. We've all been deceived by the same serpent. We've all chosen to leave the garden and enter into the desert where no water rises up from the ground to sustain us. And when we sense the weight of death pressing in, we are all driven to struggle for life. Call it our survival instinct. In the absence of God, we try to get life from other places, but no life can be found apart from him. I know this because I've looked everywhere and come up empty.

It is this empty pursuit for life that leads us into prison. If we can understand how we end up in bondage, we can also begin to find freedom.

Remember that thoughts and feelings are inextricably tied together. If we can change our thoughts, it will influence our feelings.

All this thinking and feeling does not stay bottled up in the interior world of the mind. Our inner world spills to the outside world through our bodies.

THE BODY

Obviously our bodies are the tangible part of us that everyone can see. Because we have bodies, we can interact with the physical world. All action in the body is preceded by activity in the mind. Before I smile or make a fist or walk up a flight of stairs, I've thought about it. Sometimes the activity in my mind is more pronounced and other times it is subtle.

It is true that we perform involuntary actions without thinking about them first. For example, most of the time I don't think about breathing but my lungs still take in air. However, even in this example my will and mind can exercise control over my body. I can choose to hold my breath or breathe through my nose. Each time my wife gave birth, she thought a great deal about how she was breathing.

IT GOES BOTH WAYS

I've described a linear system where the heart directs the mind and the mind directs the body. While this is all true, it is an incomplete picture. The parts in a system don't just interact in one direction. It goes both ways.

First of all, the outer world gets in through our senses. The things we see or hear or touch generate signals that move through the body and then generate thoughts and feelings in the mind. But beyond that, there is a certain boomerang effect that takes place as we move through life.

When we make a decision to think in a certain direction, which then results in a specific action, that action will generate feedback. If I experience positive thoughts and feelings after deciding to act in a certain way, I am more likely to make the same decision next time. Likewise, if an action leads to negative thoughts or emotions, I am less likely to choose the same path next time. While it is true that we can decide to go against our feelings, they do have the power to influence our decision-making ability. In other words, our resolve can be worn down.

While it is still oversimplified, we can think of this entire process as a cycle. There is constant movement, like a rolling wheel. Heart to mind, mind to body, body to mind, and mind to heart.

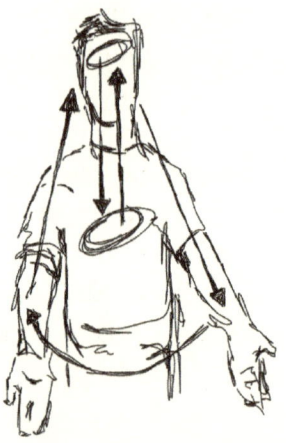

As the cycle progresses and picks up speed in a specific direction, it gets easier to keep going that way by making the same decisions and thus acting in the same ways. As less force is required to keep the cycle moving, the heart can become less active in making decisions toward certain actions. We can begin to feel like we are not choosing at all. I have a friend who says that our character is composed of the actions we take without thinking.

The process I've described is neutral. It is an explanation of how the human system works and how our choices begin to determine a course for our lives. This is how the car gets moving and keeps moving down the road. We are wired to choose the things that are good and life-giving. The question is whether the things we choose actually give life or only appear to do so.

RUNNING ON GOD

I am not the first person to compare people to car engines. C. S. Lewis wrote, "God designed the human machine to run on Himself."[2] And psychologist Gerald May explained that we've had "God's breath in us since the beginning."[3] As we saw in the first chapter, God is our life-source and he intended for us to come to him for life. Willard said that the God-intended function of the will is to reach for God.[4]

When we choose with the heart to direct our mind toward God, it puts us in close proximity to him. Then he becomes the strongest influence on our thoughts and feelings and thus our actions. When my son JJ was an infant, he used to grab onto my beard with both hands and pull my forehead into his. Heather would pick him up and he would tuck his arms in and press his head to her heart. Heather and I have largely influenced the way our kids experience reality because of their proximity to us. It works the same way with God. Practically speaking, how do we direct our minds to God? I'll describe two ways.

First, Paul said it is possible to take every thought captive (2 Corinthians 10:5). Thoughts may fly into our minds without our active participation or control, but as we saw, we can decide what to do with them. A bird once flew into our house through the front door. It landed on a high windowsill and began slamming itself into the glass. We used a long pole to nudge the bird off the windowsill and it eventually left the way it came in. When a thought enters, we can let it stay, and we can dwell on the image or the feelings that come with it. Or we can choose to send the thought away. Taking thoughts captive means chasing out destructive ideas and images, but it also means turning our attention to good things. This leads to the second way the heart can direct the mind toward God. In writing to the Philippians, Paul said, "Whatever is true, whatever is honorable, whatever is just, whatever is pure, whatever is pleasing, whatever is commendable, if there is any excellence and if there is anything worthy of praise, think about these things" (Philippians 4:8).

Paul was talking about setting the mind in a specific direction. As an act of the will, we can direct our thoughts toward God. We can choose who we allow to influence us. Paul explained this when he instructed us "to set the mind on the Spirit is life and peace" (Romans 8:6).

I recently woke up from a series of intense dreams that involved violence and persecution. As the thoughts played in my mind, I began to feel an overwhelming sense of stress and even doom. Then my mind transitioned to the image of a burning building. I was standing on a floor that was melting under my feet. All these thoughts were preventing me from falling back asleep. But as I lay there, I realized I didn't have to allow those thoughts to dominate. I made a conscious decision to stop the flames and then watched as a set of hands began to tear apart the charred remains of the building. Then I thought about those hands holding a saw and cutting fresh boards. I continued this line of thinking until the structure was rebuilt and light poured in through the windows. It did not take long to fall back asleep. Like Paul said, setting the mind on the Spirit brings life and peace.

If we allow God to direct our minds, he will also direct our actions since our actions flow from our thoughts and feelings. Good actions in the body will follow from closeness to God. These good actions generate positive activity in the mind, which reinforces the heart's decision to follow God. This is the process by which God gives us life, and the life-supply he offers never runs out because he is eternal. We can never reach the end of God. He is an infinite fuel source.

Furthermore, when our thoughts and actions are being influenced by God, we can enjoy the other good things God made in a healthy way. We can experience other people and other created things as gifts from God that point us to and remind us of the one who made them. Gerald May refers to this as the rich, open-ended existence.[5]

This is how things were meant to function. But as we know, something went wrong for all of us. The reality of the Fall means we enter this world disoriented and grow up searching for life and fulfillment apart from God. None of us started out in close proximity to God to receive his life. Instead we listen to the Deceiver and our hearts are directed in the wrong way. The serpent offers things that look good, but in reality, cannot provide us with the life we need. The choice to continue listening to him is the choice that leads us into prison.

DESCENDING INTO PRISON

Remember, we are wired to desire life. That desire should point us to God. And the truth is that there is no true life or ultimate fulfillment apart from God because all created things are limited and finite. The created world is a derivative, not a source. To continue C. S. Lewis's metaphor, living apart from God is like trying to run "on the wrong juice."[6]

But here is the problem; other sources may appear life-giving. Many things make us feel good initially and seem to fill our needs temporarily. We seek fulfillment by consuming substances, collecting possessions, or by looking to other people to validate us. Though the effect is short-lived, the initial reward is tangible and immediate. Because of this, we will pursue these things even if we know they cannot ultimately sustain us. And if we are no longer allowing God to influence our thoughts and feelings, we miss the good and lose our ability to filter out the bad. Inevitably, we become like "a city breached, without walls" (Proverbs 25:28). The thoughts and feelings entering our minds will come from anywhere and everywhere. Willard observes that the choice to move away from God leaves us "at the mercy of circumstances that evoke feelings."[7] Our decisions become mere reactions based on feelings.

When we turn to substances or people or possessions to give us life, it is like trying to drink from a hose that is disconnected from the water supply. Residual water may be left sitting in a detached hose, but it doesn't last long. As Jesus said, "everyone who drinks of this water will be thirsty again" (John 4:13).

When our thirst returns, the temptation is to keep drinking. We generally feel worse than before. This leads to an even stronger desire to find something to quench the thirst and offer some feeling of life.

BE FREE

Again, it works for a time but eventually the thirst returns.

As this process continues, we build up an internal tolerance to our "drink" of choice and our body establishes a new normal. Our cells actually become less sensitive and therefore we need larger quantities of whatever we are chasing in order to quench our thirst. We end up striving to reach a new level of normal that becomes increasingly out of reach.

The more we drink from a certain well, the more we come to depend on the water from that well. If anything blocks us or delays us from getting the thing we depend on, we actually experience stress. The body sends warning signals and the involuntary part of the brain kicks in—this is the part we don't directly control.[8]

It is true that we chose to turn away from God, which we defined as sin. We've made this choice thousands of times and we are accountable for our actions. But we also need to realize that as momentum builds in a certain direction, we make fewer and fewer active choices. Psychologists call it compulsion. It gets to the point where we are not really choosing the action. Rather we start neglecting the choice to stop. Our will goes to sleep, and we become passive. This is what Paul meant when he said that sin became active in the members of our bodies (Romans 7:5). When we've reached this level of compulsion toward certain things, a deep attachment forms.[9] We can feel an almost complete dependency on the object(s) of our attachments. This dilemma is also known as addiction. The fact that we lose control is important to see. This is part of why the idea of freedom through independence is a deception. We may think we are directing things, but we are not. As our dependency on our attachments grows, our freedom disappears.

DIFFERENT KINDS OF WATER

We are all in a different place. There are many types and levels of attachments that lead us away from God. And our various issues can have different consequences. For the sake of clarity, I will place our attachments into one of two categories, maintaining the metaphor of thirst.

Fresh Water
Some of the things that we become attached to are not inherently destructive or evil. Some of them are even gifts from God. Food, relationships, sex, and work are great examples of things that are intended for good. But when we try to draw our life, fulfillment, meaning, purpose, and/or contentment from them, they can take us into bondage. The fulfillment they provide is temporary, so we need to keep going back for more. Fresh water is healthy for us when consumed in the right way. But if we take in too much we can drown.

With these types of attachments, the destructive nature is found not so much in the object of attachment but in the attachment itself. Instead of being able to enjoy the things God made in a healthy way that points us back to him, our desire becomes misdirected, thus leading us away from him. As we latch onto the objects of our attachment, we become increasingly obsessed with acquiring the prize.

Wine, for example, is not inherently evil. Jesus turned water into wine while attending a wedding with his friends. He also used it to symbolize his sacrifice (John 2, Matthew 26). But it is also true that alcohol affects different people in different ways and when an attachment forms, it can be deadly. Sex is another example. It is a beautiful gift that is the source of life and can glue a marriage together. But when sex becomes an obsession, it can take us into very dangerous places. This leads to the second category.

Salt Water
There are other attachments and addictions we form that are inherently destructive. Illegal drugs, pornography, and gossip are good examples. With these types of attachments, it is not only that the obsession leads us away from God but also the object itself that is toxic. For example, there is not any context under which pornography can be consumed in a way that is healthy or life-giving.

One of the most difficult things about these attachments is that

BE FREE

they don't necessarily appear destructive on the surface. Just like the fresh water, they temporarily fill the void in us. But this feeling of life is a deception.

The movie *Against the Sun* retells the story of three American soldiers flying across the Pacific Ocean during World War II. As the night pressed in and darkness filled the cockpit, the pilot fell asleep. When he startled awake, he was completely disoriented and realized their fuel was almost depleted. Out of necessity, the pilot took the plane down into the water.

The three men survived the impact and managed to pull themselves into the life raft. Within a few days, they became delirious from dehydration. The deception of the sea was powerful. These thirsty men were bobbing in the middle of an ocean. The only thing they could see was water. The longer they dried up, the more the salt water looked like life. Because of their desperate thirst, the salt water would have brought some relief at first. The problem is that it would have left them even closer to death in the end.

WHAT ALL SIN HAS IN COMMON

The implications of sin will vary depending on both the type and the degree of our attachments. Having acknowledged that, it is important to note that all sin has common traits, regardless of the particulars. A person may feel they are doing "pretty good" compared to the next person, and therefore may feel less urgency to change. They may be tempted to dismiss their own sins. This will keep a person in denial about their need for liberation.

Internal vs. External
Our hearts ultimately direct our minds and our minds take us into action. In other words, the things I do with my body flow from the inside out. This means that sin is first an internal problem that involves motives and thoughts. I could carry out what appears to be a good action, but do so with a self-serving motive. Jesus confronted the

religious leaders for trying to appear generous in order to gain the praises of people (Matthew 6:2).

I could also engage in destructive thoughts that would not be detected by an outside observer. Paul said that to set the mind on the flesh is death (Romans 8:6). And Jesus said that lust is the same as adultery and anger is equivalent to murder (Matthew 5:20–30). While the lustful glance is less obvious than a physical affair, the thoughts and motives behind each are related. And while some of the sins we struggle with may seem hidden and therefore "feel" less serious, they are not hidden from God. As the Old Testament author wrote, our hearts lie open before God (Proverbs 15:11).

Lawlessness Leads to More Lawlessness
Sin is not self-limiting, but has a progression to it. It is possible for us to fall deeper and deeper into our bondage. Seeking life apart from God is like rolling down a hill. Things can escalate and accelerate quickly. In Romans, Paul discussed how lawlessness leads to more lawlessness, or to greater and greater iniquity (Romans 6:19).

Occasional lust, for example, can easily lead someone into pornography, which can lead to more serious things. I once saw a nightly news special where a media team set up a sting operation to lure child predators. The organizers posed as underage girls and initiated on-line conversations with men. The "girl" would communicate her age and eventually invite the man to her house for a sexual encounter—usually stating that her parents were gone. When the perpetrators arrived at the house, cameras and police were there to meet them inside. I don't know the individual stories of these men. But I do know they didn't start out as forty-year-old men who would be willing to solicit fourteen-year-old girls. They probably struggled with lust early on (like most adolescent boys, including me). This may have led to consuming images of women on a glossy cover or screen. Eventually, the screen was not enough. With each step, they climbed farther into the prison of lust until they lost all discernment and knew only a deep, consuming thirst for sex.

BE FREE

Gateway Drugs

This final idea is closely related to the previous one. It is true that some attachments and sins seem less serious or threatening than others. However, these attachments can still be harmful in a more indirect way because they can wear down our defenses, making us vulnerable to more serious things.

Sugar, for example, is an attachment that I struggle with quite a bit. I'll be the first to admit that cupcakes don't seem all that dangerous. However, one thing that is important to consider about sugar is that it provides almost instant gratification (some say it impacts the brain in a similar manner to cocaine). The more I try to get satisfaction from eating sugar, the more I program my body to expect a quick fix. Author David Wolfe identifies a phenomenon he calls "the sugar drug culture." He explains that when we receive quick gratification from sugar and other substances, it can set us up to expect this result in other areas of life as well. A general predisposition to instant gratification can easily lead to other attachments.[10]

LOSING OUR CAPACITY TO LOVE

Thus far we have looked at how sin takes us into slavery. However, something more destructive can result from sin. It is not just how our sin changes us, but how it impacts those around us. Here, we begin to see the true evil of sin. The more consumed we become with feeding the monster inside, the less concern we have for other people (compassion is a limited resource for us without God's Spirit). As our attachments grow and multiply, we form an increasingly inward focus. This implosion of the heart makes it nearly impossible to love God and to love people. In essence, we begin to lose the capacity to love.[11]

As we lose our ability to love, we lose the point of living. As previously stated, love is the whole point. It is why God created us. This loss of purpose brings destruction and brokenness to our relationships. It happens in two main ways.

Neglected

The self-seeking quality of sin inevitably causes us to become blind to those around us—especially to those who are not able or willing to provide us with something we want. This is sometimes referred to as the sin of omission. Rather than taking actions that are wrong, we often neglect to do the right thing.

Not long ago I became aware of a way that my sin was causing me to neglect the person closest to me. One night my wife and I were sitting in the living room talking about the day. She asked me if I'd remembered to fix the blinds. Our kids like to throw balls in the basement and the family room blinds were in rough shape. Heather had asked me more than once to repair the damage. Not only had I forgotten to fix the blinds, but I immediately got defensive when I sensed she felt hurt by my neglect. An argument began which involved me making sure Heather knew there are other husbands out there who are far worse than me. The discussion ended, as it often would, with Heather going quiet and me going into a different room to pray and sort out why I'd reacted that way.

This may seem like a small thing, but I became aware that something profound was taking place. Heather and I had been in many fights like this one. The truth is, I have often neglected to do things that were important to Heather. Finally, God showed me the reason. The neglect was not an intentional dismissal of her feelings. Instead, I realized that I'd been using my work to gain world affirmation and, therefore, life apart from God. As a result, my attention and effort were mostly focused on doing good work (even when I wasn't at work). The bi-product was that I continually forgot to do the unseen jobs at home that would not generate the same level of praise.

When this pattern of neglect is carried out to further extremes in our lives, it leads to even more serious issues, like greed. If I am trying to gain fulfillment through my possessions and through piling up resources, I will be far more likely to hoard those resources—even at the expense of others who are under-resourced. I would argue that the mass poverty facing our world is largely due to sins of omission. It is the result of our neglect.

BE FREE

While sin can lead us to overlook each other, it can also lead us to harm each other in a more direct way.

Used and Abused
The next way that we harm each other because of sin is through use and abuse. If we are honest, many of our relationships are at least partially motivated by what we can gain from the other person. In a healthy relationship, both sides give and receive, which is beautiful. But receiving is different than taking. Because of sin, our relationships can become distorted and we may give with the motive of receiving. It comes down to using another person to gain life.

To go a step further, we also tend to abuse one another. If another person refuses to give us what we want, or gets in the way of what we want, the sinful heart will often lash out. We can see this when young children hit each other with wooden blocks and when we adults argue at the top of our lungs. Early in my marriage, my wife and I were having an argument. At one point, I became so upset that I actually shoved a chair into a set of cabinets, causing the chair to break. My wife went for a drive to give us both a break, and I remember sitting on the floor of the garage trying to glue the chair back together. In that moment, I was very aware of the impact sin has on our relationships.

Just as with neglect, the tendency for human beings to use and abuse one another has taken us to some very dark extremes. Throughout human history, sex has been worshiped as a god and the victims of this distorted worship have been sacrificed on the altar. This isn't an ancient or remote phenomenon. The sex slave industry is more massive today than any other time in history. Though a victim may be used in a hotel room on the Vegas strip instead of a temple, it is still part of the same devastating sickness.

Another example of how we use and abuse others is murder. We are accustomed to stories of people killing one another for drugs or money or religion. I even heard a story of a man who shot a relative over a TV remote. Human history has been driven by one war after another. Every time a new conflict breaks out, each side believes they are fighting for a valid reason. Often, the reason is either that the

BOBBING IN THE MIDDLE OF AN OCEAN

other side has something they want, or the other side is trying to take something they have. Some wars have been fought for nobler causes, but extreme acts of violence often come down to placing greater value on certain things or people over others. The biggest problem with violence is that it never ends. The losing side generally ends up with more reason to strike back in the future.

MORE TO THE STORY

It is important that we come to terms with what has happened to us as a result of our sin. We must take responsibility for the things we've done and failed to do. There is no point in continuing to live in denial of our prison. It is not helpful. Having said that, we also need to realize there is more to the story. Here are two points to consider.

First, while we have all caused pain to others, we've also had pain inflicted upon us. We've all neglected and abused others but we've also been neglected and abused. We all carry brokenness because of things that we had no control over, because of sins committed against us. This brokenness adds bricks to our prison walls. Unfortunately, the wounds we carry often lead us into further sin because we are seeking escape from the pain. Our sin and our brokenness play off each other and leave us in a tangled mess. This is not meant to excuse our sin, but it is vital to realize that not everything is solely our fault. There is a shared responsibility among all of humanity for the condition we are in. This speaks to the magnitude of the sin problem.

The second point concerns our origin. Despite how bad things have gotten, the beginning of our story was good! We were born to live in the Garden of Eden, where we used to walk with God. That is who we were meant to be. In discussing the Fall, C. S. Lewis said that the original man was truly a "son of God" and, of course, the woman was truly a daughter. Lewis continues that if we were to encounter these original people before they fell, we would likely "fall at [their] feet"[12] because they carried the image of God in an untarnished form. The problem is, our fall took us a long way down. Paul said we were dead through [our] trespasses and sins" (Ephesians 2:1). And after spending enough time in darkness and death, it changed us.

I will never forget the first time I saw the character Gollum in the movie *The Lord of the Rings*. His wiry hair greased to his large head, which was held up by a bony frame. His flesh deteriorated and his skin pickled. It was hard to look at him. But he hadn't always looked that way. He was once a hobbit. He was like a man with health in his bones and life in his face. Gollum's sickly, evil appearance was something he'd acquired. The outward decay of his body was a visible manifestation of what had happened to his heart because of greed. But he was meant for something better.

Remembering that we have a good beginning to our story is vital because it means there is hope we could find goodness again. And realizing we are part of a problem that is bigger than us is important because it means, if we are going to find that goodness, we need a solution that is bigger than us. Thankfully, God has provided one. Our job is to learn to trust him.

TROUBLE TRUSTING

So how does God respond to our sin? Has he already responded? Many of us believe God is either indifferent toward us or angry with us. In other words, he has either washed his hands of us or aims to punish us because of sin. Both are lies. The glorious truth is that he loves us and came to rescue and redeem us. He made a way for us to be free and to be good again.

However, before we can get to the good news, we have to address these negative pictures of God. They run deep for many of us and if we don't uproot them, we will have trouble trusting God. And if we don't trust him, we won't take the hand he is offering, which means we won't experience the freedom he wants to give us.

CHAPTER 3

BAD DADS
CHANGING OUR PICTURE OF GOD

PICTURES OF GOD

We all have a mental picture of God. This picture is a good indicator of how we relate to him. To show you what I mean, try this simple exercise: Close your eyes and picture God. Now write down what you saw and what feelings came with the mental image.

It's possible that your picture of God feels more like a mist or a faint smoke than a person. Maybe you sometimes question whether God exists at all and so you see an empty room where the only sound is the hum of electricity in the fluorescent lights. This God feels impersonal or possibly non-existent.

Or maybe your image of God is based on someone from your life. I know of a man whose father lost his job and turned to alcohol. He didn't become angry, he just disappeared. This man's father would spend hours alone in his garage drinking. If God is anything like this, you can see his silhouette through the window of the garage, but he never comes around or pays attention to you.

When I used to think of God, I would see myself lying on the floor of the Sistine Chapel looking up. In this picture, God wore a bed sheet and had long, white hair that flowed into his beard so there was no distinction between the hair on his head and on his face. This God floated over me on a pile of angels and stretched out his long arm with a pointed finger that could either make a person or shoot out a lightning bolt. His expression was cold, possibly even angry. Once when I was praying, I became aware I was envisioning a throne where all I could see were the giant, sandaled feet of God. The face wasn't just cold, it was absent.

BE FREE

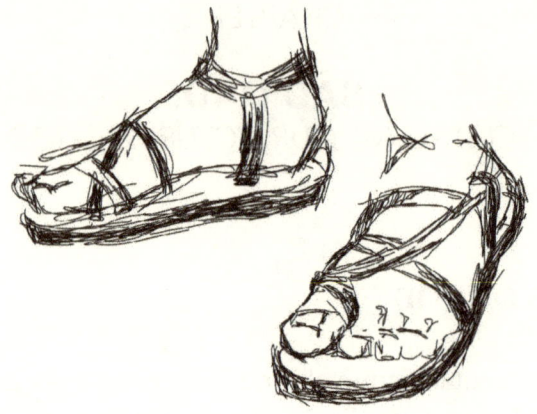

What is important is not so much the picture but what it represents. The "garage God" is absent and unable or unwilling to help. The "ceiling God" is strong but in your face, ready to bring down discipline. The problem is, if our view of God is negative, it is unlikely we'll turn to him or trust him. Instead we will hold tight to our independence and, as a result, won't experience freedom.

For the sake of discussion, we could place the negative views of God on a spectrum that ranges from indifferent to angry. None of these views lead us into a relationship with him. Thankfully, these views are not an accurate depiction of him. God is not indifferent, and he is not angry. The truth is that God is good. He is love (1 John 4:16). But to believe this, we need to address the negative views we may have of God and expose them as lies.

GOD IS NEVER IN FRANCE

Many people believe God has simply checked out, and that he looks at us with cold indifference. One expression of this is Deism. It is the view that God created the universe but then moved on, allowing it to keep running without his involvement or concern.

This reminds me of a scene in the movie *The Count of Monte Cristo* where the hero, Edmond, first arrives in prison after being falsely accused and convicted. The warden and a couple of guards lead him to his cell, and then take his chains and attach them to an anchor in the wall. The men pull the chains taut, causing Edmond's arms to lift and stretch. As the warden rips the shirt from his back, Edmond realizes they are about to beat him. He then speaks to the warden about God. The warden listens with a calm, almost happy expression, as though he is getting ready to play a game. As the warden rolls up his sleeves, he responds by saying, "God is never in France this time of year . . ." That was the beginning of a seventeen-year incarceration during which the reality of God eroded from Edmond's heart.

The idea of an indifferent God has been around for a long time. In one of the Psalms, David wrote, "I cry aloud to God, aloud to God, that he may hear me . . . Will the Lord spurn forever, and never again be favorable? Has his steadfast love ceased forever? Are his promises at an end for all time?" (Psalm 77:1, 7–8).

Though David was a friend of God, in times of struggle, he seemed to believe God had abandoned him. We often do the same thing. But what causes us to believe God is indifferent toward us? A couple of things feed into this idea.

First, when we consider our own struggle with sin, many of us just assume that God will want nothing to do with us. Perhaps we've experienced judgment from other people around our particular area of sin. Or maybe we've felt excluded from a church because of our past. Human beings tend to shun each other and we can often, then, attribute this characteristic to God. The truth is, God does not shun us because of our sin. The next chapter examines how he actually chooses to pursue us in spite of our sin.

But there is a second reason I believe we accuse God of being indifferent, and it has to do with the sins committed against us. We reason that if God cared about us, he would prevent people from doing bad things to us. The problem is, for God to take such an action, he would need to take away our freedom.

A while back, I was arguing with God. It was on a day when I was very aware of evil in the world. After hearing about a serious terrorist attack overseas, I saw another story on the news about a young mother killed in her home by a stranger. As I was driving home, I was angry. I literally yelled at God, "Why don't you stop them?!" At that moment, God gave me a picture. I saw a vision of kids playing soccer in an alley.

I sensed the Holy Spirit saying this was a picture of the terrorists when they were younger. Then he said that in order to stop them, he would have needed to kill them there in the alley; because the terrorist attack was actually the result of countless choices over a lifetime. Next, I saw a cresting river that sent a torrent of water through the alley. I felt like God asked rhetorically, "Why stop here?" It quickly became clear to me what the Holy Spirit was trying to show me. For God to intervene in the way I wanted him to, he would have to eliminate anyone who might choose to sin and cause suffering to others. This would mean removing everyone—including me.

We want justice and we want God to prevent bad things from happening in advance. We feel if he were a loving God, he would drop his hand down like a wall to block every tragedy before it hits. We need to realize this would require God to revoke the freedom he gave us.

C. S. Lewis said it like this. "[The] permanent nature of wood which enables us to use it as a beam also enables us to use it for hitting our neighbor on the head."[1] In other words, we live in a world that is set up to allow people (and angels) to freely choose either right or wrong. If God was going to prevent every bad thing that happened in this type of a world, he would have to turn the piece of wood into a blade of grass in the hand of the angry person. Or he would have to grab the wood beam from the person's hand, drive it into the ground, and tie the offender to the post by his or her hands and feet. In other words, God would have to revoke the freedom of every guilty person. This means he would have to revoke all freedom, and thus, choosing who or what we love would cease to exist. God didn't give us freedom just because he wants us to love him, but also because he loves us.

My oldest son Sam once suffered a compound fracture in his arm. This happened while my wife and I were sitting in the same room, a few feet away. We had our back to him working on something. He was playing rough and rolled over his arm. When we turned to see what had happened, his arm was in the shape of an "S." The break was so bad the bone had poked through the skin.

Thinking back, I wondered if we could have prevented the injury. He was doing something we had instructed him not to do, but our council hadn't prevented him from doing it. The only thing I can figure is that we could have chosen to keep him on house arrest and forced him to wear one of those giant bubble suits at all times. But the moment I say that, it is clear that this action would be the opposite of love. Freedom is required to love but love also requires that we grant freedom. To imprison a person is not loving.

Because God loves us and wants us to be able to reciprocate his love, he must allow for our freedom. He must allow for the possibility of sin. There is no other way about it. This is why God does not revoke our ability to choose.

While this is true, it is so much easier to speak of theoretically rather than practically. In the midst of suffering, especially when we are suffering because of someone else's sin, the heart's response is to scoff at freedom. These ideas may not help remove the sting of suffering, but they can help us interpret suffering in a way that draws us closer to God rather than driving us away.

The truth is, God is not indifferent toward sin. He is involved and has chosen to respond to our condition. Before we can look at God's true reaction to our sin, we need to dissolve a couple more misconceptions.

BE FREE

AN ENABLER?

We said in the beginning we often think of freedom as the right to do whatever we want. I believe that some of us want this degree of freedom and then unconsciously (or subconsciously) believe God should intervene by bailing us out when our choices get us in trouble. There are two problems with this view.

First, if God were to respond by simply removing the consequences of our choices, he would still be canceling out freedom. In the book *Satan and the Problem of Evil*, Greg Boyd explained something he called the "irrevocability" of freedom. He wrote, "God allows [us] to endure as decision-making agents in the course [we] choose for [ourselves]."[2] In other words, if we are really free, we must be allowed to experience the results of our choices. If God lifted the natural consequences of human choice every time we acted outside of his will, then we would have never been free to begin with. Our freedom would only be an illusion.

Second, and perhaps more importantly, if we didn't have to be accountable for our actions, we would never change how we behaved and therefore, would perpetuate evil through our sin. It would be as though God were giving us license to sin.

When I was in high school, I was in a car accident. My dad was driving our van, and I was sitting in the front passenger seat. Our neighbor was sitting next to my older sister in the middle seats of the vehicle. As my dad headed south down the highway, a truck crossed the road. (I never saw the truck before he hit us so I have to reconstruct those couple of seconds from my imagination.) The sound of crashing metal is the first thing I remember. It was so blunt and loud my brain couldn't process what had happened. Our van rolled and slid into a bed of weeds in the ditch and we were left hanging by our seat belts.

I don't remember who called the police or if we even had cell phones back then. In a matter of minutes, we were encircled by flashing lights and men with small notebooks. The police determined immediately that the young man driving the truck was one hundred percent at fault.

The other person who arrived on the scene was the father of the young man who'd hit us. It was not unusual that his father came, but I will always be amazed by what happened next. Within a few minutes of arriving, the father handed his own car keys to his son. Then, the son got into his father's car and drove off while the father stayed to talk with the police. I believe this man was trying to help his son. But the truth is, he was simply enabling him, which, in the end, causes harm. A few months later, the same driver hit another car on the way to school.

By trying to erase the consequences for a person's destructive choices, we allow them to continue down the same road. Some may say we are even empowering them to do more damage. A blanket acquittal with no accountability does not resolve the problem of sin.

An alternative response on the part of God would be for him to become angry with our choices. This is probably one of the most prominent views about how God responds to sin and it, too, needs to be deconstructed so we can begin to trust again.

ARROWS OF THE ALMIGHTY

Many believe that God responds to our sin by punishing. Perhaps one of the strongest champions of the angry God view was a preacher named Jonathan Edwards. In 1741, he preached a sermon called "Sinners in the Hands of an Angry God." This sermon became a famous piece of American literature and it represents a way of thinking that has influenced how society views God.

Edwards spoke about a God who was ready at every moment to vent his wrath. He wrote, "The Sword of divine Justice is every Moment brandished over their Heads, and 'tis nothing but the Hand of arbitrary Mercy, and God's mere Will, that holds it back." He also described a bow in tension with the "Arrow made ready on the String."[3] The weapon was apparently aimed at the guilty parties. Edwards believed that when God looked at humanity, it was with one eye closed and the other staring down the shaft of an arrow.

While he was a loud voice, Jonathan Edwards was not the first person who communicated this view of God. One of the earliest examples of this view comes directly from the book of Job.

Job was a man who experienced immense suffering. Those around him assumed that his suffering must be punishment from God for some sin he had committed. His friend Eliphaz said, "As I have seen, those who plow iniquity and sow trouble reap the same. By the breath of God they perish, and by the blast of his anger they are consumed" (Job 4:8–9). But we learn that Job was not suffering because of sin. In fact, God himself confirmed that Job was a blameless and upright man (Job 1:8).

In reality, Job was suffering because of a battle being fought over him in the spiritual realm. Satan accused God of being coercive—implying that Job only loved God because he'd been given material wealth. Satan then asked permission to attack Job to see if he would reject God when the blessings were removed. The fact that Satan (whose name means *adversary*) confronted God is evidence that he possessed freedom of choice (just like humans do). Author James Morgenstern wrote that the adversary presented in this story had "become semi-independent of God, a true, creative power and source of evil in the world…"[4] In other words, Satan was asking to exercise the freedom that God had already granted him, and God chose not to revoke it. If God had simply obliterated Satan, it would have confirmed the demonic accusation that God was controlling and coercive toward his people/creation. Again, to remove freedom is to undermine love.

We are told that Satan had to leave God's presence where he acted in his own "power" to afflict Job (Job 1:6–12). The story confirms that Satan had the freedom to act and he clearly used this power to harm God's faithful. He was even directly identified as the one who inflicted Job's body with sores (Job 2:7).

Because Job wasn't aware that the attacks on his life were from Satan, he thought God was the one afflicting him. And because Job didn't believe he was guilty of sin, the affliction seemed arbitrary. In one of Job's speeches, he accused God of being the adversary (Job 16:9); he believed God had pierced him with an arrow. Job said, "The arrows of the Almighty are in me, my spirit drinks in their poison; the terrors of God are arrayed against me" (Job 6:4).

If we were to pull Job's words out of context, we may start to believe God is angry, just like Edwards believed. But when we look at the whole story, we can see that Job was mistaken. He was acting on bad assumptions. When Job had finally finished talking, God offered a response. He didn't crush Job with a storm, but he did speak to him from the storm. God said to Job: "Who is this that darkens counsel by words without knowledge? Gird up your loins like a man, I will question you, and you shall declare to me 'Where were you when I laid the foundation of the earth? Tell me, if you have understanding'" (Job 38:2–4).

God was basically saying that there were things going on that Job had no knowledge of. While God never provided Job with a complete explanation, he did at least refer to a hidden battle that was being waged. God spoke to Job about a creature called Leviathan. This being was a spectacle of power and fury. Its back was covered with scales like shields, and its chest was like a rock. Leviathan spit out fire, and smoke streamed from his nostrils. We are told this being was king over the proud and no one could subdue him—no one but God (Job 40–41). In Psalm 74:14 the writer tells us that God is the only one who can crush the head of Leviathan.

The imagery of this powerful, serpent-like creature was common in the ancient Near Eastern world, used as a means of describing the powers of chaos and evil in the world.⁵ When we consider this cultural context and the references to Satan as the adversary in the beginning of Job, it is reasonable to make a connection between Satan and Leviathan. In the words of Greg Boyd, "Satan was himself Leviathan."⁶ In an indirect way, God was confirming that Satan was the archer who was afflicting Job with arrows. Paul echoed this in Ephesians when he wrote about the "flaming arrows of the evil one" (6:16).

After his conversation with God, Job repented and admitted that he had spoken about things he didn't understand (Job 42:1–6). He realized his angry picture of God was a lie. As the psalmist wrote, God is "slow to anger and abounding in steadfast love" (Psalm 103:8).

Despite the claims of Job's friends, the story of Job does not provide us with a picture of God who is angry at humanity because of sin. In fact, God specifically said they were wrong to suggest this (Job 42:7). It does, however, provide us with a picture of God who wages war against the forces that contribute to our sin and destruction. He is the one who can crush the head of Leviathan. God is not angry with us because of sin, but he is fierce toward sin because it separates us from his love.

And this brings us to the point where we can finally discuss how God responds to our sin. He does not excuse it, nor does he punish it. Instead he launched an invasion against the kingdom of darkness in order to destroy it. This invasion was called the Incarnation.

CHAPTER 4

THE LION WHO BECAME A LAMB
HOW JESUS SETS US FREE

Near the end of the Lewis classic *The Lion, the Witch and the Wardrobe*, is a scene where Aslan returns to the witch's castle after having just resurrected. He leaps over the wall with the girls on his back and they land in the middle of a courtyard filled with statues. The statues were once living creatures. But the witch had taken them captive and held them in prison by turning them into stone with her dark magic. As the girls watch, Aslan walks up to the first statue, which is also a lion. He breathes on the stone lion and at first nothing changes. But then something starts to happen. Lewis wrote,

> The color seemed to lick all over him as the flame licks all over a bit of paper—then, while his hindquarters were still obviously stone, the lion shook his mane and all the heavy, stone folds rippled into living hair. Then he opened a great red mouth, warm and living, and gave a prodigious yawn.[1]

BE FREE

The good news of Christianity is ultimately about a great rescue followed by redemption. Humanity was captive to Satan, sin, and death. We were a race of stone statues, standing frozen in the prison yard. But God intervened to destroy the kingdom of darkness and set us free. This intervention came when God sent his own son to save us (John 3:16).

John told us that Jesus was in the beginning with God (John 1:1). In other words, his existence did not start with his birth. He was not created or derived. In fact, he helped with creation (John 1:3). He is eternal, just like God the Father. They, along with the Holy Spirit, have existed in relationship with one another since the beginning.

But the Bible also teaches that Jesus left heaven and came to earth. The mystery of the Incarnation is discussed in Paul's letter to the Philippians. "Let the same mind be in you that was in Christ Jesus, who, though he was in the form of God, did not regard equality with God as something to be exploited, but emptied himself, taking on the form of a slave, being born in human likeness. And being found in human form…" (Philippians 2:5–7).

Jesus, who shares in the divine nature of God the Father, willingly chose to set aside certain aspects of his divinity that would be inconsistent with being human (i.e. he emptied himself). John explained that Jesus "descended" (3:13). Scholars refer to this idea as *kenosis*, which means to lay aside.[2] So, for example, God is omnipresent (in all places at once), but one limitation of being human is that we can only be present in one place at a time.

Though he temporarily set aside these aspects of divinity, he retained the full essence of God, which is love. In other words, he was still divine. Jesus didn't just represent the Father like an ambassador—he actually revealed the Father. Jesus said to his friends, "Whoever has seen me has seen the Father" (John 14:9). Later, the Jesus followers said he was, "the exact imprint of God's very being" and the "image of the invisible God" (Hebrews 1:3, Colossians 1:15). Paul said that in Jesus "the whole fullness of deity dwells bodily" (Colossians 2:9). In Jesus, we are able to see the full nature of God in a body.

THE LION WHO BECAME A LAMB

So, he was human, but he was also God. I have a mentor who often refers to Jesus as the God-man. This idea is consistent with the story of Jesus' birth. He entered the world through Mary's womb but was conceived by the power of the Holy Spirit (Matthew 1:18). An angel spoke to Joseph, who was betrothed to Mary, and called the new baby "Emmanuel," which means "God is with us" (Matthew 1:23). Like I said, he is the God-man.

We should not overlook that he entered the world by entering a womb. If the Incarnation was an invasion against the kingdom of darkness, we would expect God to ride in on an iron horse with smoke streaming from its nostrils. We would expect him to come as a full-grown man suited in armor that clapped loudly against his body as he rode. But instead, God came as a baby.

COMING TO A DANGEROUS PLACE

Being born is a risky endeavor. The birth process is delicate, and it is amazing that a fetus can grow and survive to reach full term. And then, of course, babies are the most vulnerable members of the human family, because this fallen world is a dangerous place to visit.

My family and I were once walking to the park on a warm day. I was watching the streamers on my daughter's handlebars flapping against her elbows when a black, European car passed us traveling well over the speed limit. I could feel the wind as it passed. I was angry because a kid on a bike and a speeding car can be a fatal combination. Then Ellie stopped and picked up some flowers lying on the sidewalk. They were drooping and dead. At the park, we passed some berries that I think were poisonous and we also saw a mouse along the path that had been hit by a bike. Small flies hovered around it.

As beautiful as this world is, it is also filled with danger. Death, or the threat of death, is a common phenomenon, even in places that seem safe. I am not being fatalistic—just stating a fact. In the Incarnation, the vast and powerful God became a baby. In doing so, he exposed himself to the reality of physical pain and even death.

BE FREE

As Philip Yancey says, "A mule could have stepped on him."[3]

Shortly after his birth, he was confronted by the threat of King Herod, who was in power in Jerusalem at the time of Jesus' birth. When Herod heard that this new baby was being called the king of the Jews, he killed all the children in and around Bethlehem who were two years old or younger. Jesus survived because Mary and Joseph escaped to Egypt after being warned in a dream (Matthew 2:1–18).

Though it is not generally read at Christmas, Revelation 12 refers to the same event described by Matthew. "Then the dragon stood before the woman who was about to bear a child, so that he might devour her child as soon as it was born." John wrote that this child, who would rule the nations, was snatched away from the dragon.

In light of this, the danger of Jesus' birth is unmistakable. And while the confrontation started with his birth, it shifted into full force when he became a man. After being baptized by his cousin, Jesus went into the wilderness where he was tempted by the devil. He tried to test Jesus and even offered him the kingdoms of the world (which he apparently still had some authority over), but Jesus resisted and rejected every offer. He told the enemy that he lived by every word that came from the mouth of God and that he would worship God alone (Matthew 4:1–11). Jesus faced Satan but he did not fall.

In fact, he faced every temptation we face, and yet he didn't sin. The writer of Hebrews said, "[W]e have one who in every respect has been tested [or tempted] as we are, yet without sin" (4:15). In other words, Jesus felt the same pull toward sin that we do. But the difference is, he remained faithful and lived in perfect unity with the Father—even unto his death (Hebrews 12:4). In this way, he was the opposite of Adam (and all of us). Our disobedience gave the enemy a hold in this world but because of Jesus' obedience, Satan had no power over him (Romans 5:17, John 14:30). Jesus showed what it looks like for a human being to reject the lie of independence and receive true life from the Father. Jesus' obedience began the process of unraveling the kingdom of darkness. But Jesus didn't just resist evil, he launched an attack against it.

THE LION WHO BECAME A LAMB

REBUKING WAVES AND WAKING PEOPLE UP

When he left the wilderness, Jesus came out proclaiming that the kingdom of God had come to earth (Matthew 4:17). He further clarified his mission when he stood up in the synagogue and read from the prophet Isaiah:

> The spirit of the Lord God is upon me, because the Lord has anointed me; he has sent me to bring good news to the oppressed, to bind up the brokenhearted, to proclaim liberty to the captives, and release to the prisoners; to proclaim the year of the Lord's favor, and the day of vengeance of our God; to comfort all who mourn. —Isaiah 61:1–2

When he finished reading, he told the people that the words of the prophet had been fulfilled in their hearing (Luke 4:16–21). The words were about him. He was foretelling that his mission was to liberate captives and to heal the brokenhearted. He came to dismantle sin and bring liberation and healing to all who were bound and broken by it. His ministry was an offensive mission against dark spiritual forces. And as you read the gospel stories, you can sense a building or a swelling taking place in this battle. Consider the following collection of stories from the gospel of Luke.

Jesus was once crossing a lake with his followers. He had fallen asleep when a storm rose up. The men were afraid and woke Jesus. He got up and Luke tells us he rebuked the wind and the raging waves. Instantly they were calm and his followers marveled at the fact that the storm seemed to obey Jesus (Luke 8:22–25). The word for "rebuke" in this story is *epitimao*. It can mean to warn, redirect, prevent, or place due weight upon. The interesting thing is that this is the same word that was often used when Jesus confronted demons to send them away from people (Matthew 17:18, Luke 4:35). While it is an inference, some have reasoned that the rebuking of the storm and the obedient response of the weather could indicate a dark spiritual force behind the storm. This point becomes even more probable when we look at where Jesus was going.

In the story that follows, Jesus stepped onto land in the country of the Gerasenes, and he encountered a man who was bound by demons. The man had no clothes and he did not live in a house. Instead, he had been living in the tombs. He was often chained, but when the demons seized him, he would break the bonds and be driven out into the wild. Everything about this story speaks of death. The man was like a walking corpse. But Jesus moved directly into this death and commanded these forces to leave the man. He freed the man, though not without a concentrated effort, because the evil holding him was vast and powerful (Luke 8:26–39).

After leaving this man, Jesus went back across the lake and encountered death again. A man named Jairus approached him and explained that his daughter was dying. He begged Jesus to help. On his way to the man's house, a bleeding woman stopped Jesus. She had been hemorrhaging for twelve years, and no one could help her. The woman touched the fringe of Jesus' clothes and the bleeding stopped immediately. It was as though his robe was soaked with power, and he felt the healing as it happened. Jesus stopped to engage with the woman and affirm her faith. Though Luke doesn't mention it specifically in this story, there was often a connection made between physical healing and deliverance from demonic oppression (Luke 13:10–16).

Finally, Jesus transitions from confronting Satan to confronting death itself. While he was still speaking, someone came from the house of the dying girl and explained she was gone. But Jesus was not deterred and he continued to the house. When he arrived, he reassured everyone the girl was only sleeping. The people laughed at him, thinking he was confused, but Jesus was not ignorant about death, he was simply not defeated by it. Jesus took her hand and called her out of the fatal rest (Luke 8:49–55).

All the gospel accounts read this way. Jesus moved around and everyone who was sick or demonized was pulled toward him like debris in a strong tide. He reversed the power of Satan and death everywhere he went. Eventually it came time for the final confrontation with death at which time an important shift took place. Rather than resisting death, Jesus allowed himself to be killed.

LAYING DOWN HIS OWN LIFE

Near the end of his time on earth, Jesus began to prepare his friends for what was about to happen to him. He explained that he was going to undergo great suffering and that he would be killed. His friends did not want to hear this. Peter actually rebuked Jesus, declaring it must never happen. In response, Jesus turned to Peter and said, "Get behind me, Satan! You are a stumbling block to me; for you are setting your mind not on divine things but on human things" (Matthew 16:23). Jesus' response to Peter seems strong, but it reveals that Jesus was approaching his death with fierce intention. He was adamant that his death was necessary. Though he didn't know it at the time, Peter would later understand why.

The reality of his approaching death was further confirmed when a woman came to Jesus with a jar of costly ointment and poured it on his head. Jesus explained that the woman had done a good thing and that she had anointed his body for its burial (Mark 14:3–8).

The accounts of Jesus' execution further confirm that his plan all along was to willingly subject himself to death. Satan eventually entered one of Jesus' followers, named Judas, and led him to betray Jesus (Luke 22:3). Judas led an angry mob to Jesus in order to arrest him. Again, one of his friends tried to intervene and cut off the ear of someone in the mob. But Jesus stopped him and then reattached the man's ear with his hands (Luke 22:51).

After instructing Peter to put down his weapon, Jesus said, "Do you think that I cannot appeal to my Father, and he will at once send me more than twelve legions of angels?" (Matthew 26:53). The implication is that God could have summoned a literal army of angels to descend on the earth and eliminate those opposing him. He could have not only taken out the mob, Jesus could have put an end to the entire Roman army with one prayer. But he chose not to. Instead of killing those guilty of evil, he chose to die in their place.

After allowing himself to be taken away, Jesus stood mostly silent before those accusing him (Matthew 27:12–14). Finally, the religious and political leaders, under the deceit of the evil one, sentenced Jesus to death and executed him. I use the word "deceived" because Jesus said they didn't understand what they were doing (Luke 23:34). Satan used human beings like sharp tools in his cold fingers. He is like a mob leader who makes others do the killing. Paul said that the devil holds people captive to do his will (2 Timothy 2:26).

The main point in all of this is that Jesus allowed it. He said to those killing him, "You would have no power over me unless it had been given you from above..." (John 19:11). The implication is that he and the Father (remember, they are one) planned on this trial and execution. He took our violence and the violence of the enemy upon himself.

But why would God allow himself to be killed? No one understood. His friends were devastated and scattered (Mark 14:50). This was not what they wanted. They wanted God to intervene, but not in this way. They wanted him to sweep Rome off the planet, like he was clearing a table with a mighty arm. They wanted their oppressors to shatter on the ground like dishes. But God dying . . . that wasn't supposed to happen. It was harsh and fast—like water thrown on a fire, their leader snuffed out. As they listened to the hissing of drenched wood and as they breathed in the wet smoke, they believed it was over.

Again, we might ask why? Why the cross? Paul said that Jesus erased the record against us and that it was nailed to the cross (Colossians 2:14). He was explaining that through Jesus' death on the cross, he destroyed the power of sin. To understand why the cross destroys sin, we need to first understand how the cross was an act of love.

Jesus said there is no greater love than to lay down one's life for a friend (John 15:13). I once heard a story about an old man in an active shooter situation. When he saw the gunman, he jumped on top of his wife. He took three bullets in the back but saved her life in the process.

But somehow, Jesus surpassed even this. Because he did not only lay down his life for his friends—he also died for those who counted him an enemy. Paul said that the sinful mind is "hostile to God" (Romans 8:7)

THE LION WHO BECAME A LAMB

and it was while we were still sinners that Christ died for us (Romans 5:8). So, he sacrificed himself for us while we still lived in hostility toward him. And if all of this were not enough, he didn't just suffer physical pain and death.

The Bible says that Jesus became sin so that we could become the righteousness of God (2 Corinthians 5:21). If Jesus became sin it means that he knew the experience of spiritual death. Sin separates us from God, which causes us to die spiritually. We broke the covenant and earned death (Romans 6:23). But he took the responsibility for our sin and died in our place. Part of the Godhead allowed himself to undergo the experience of God-forsakenness. On the cross, he called out to the Father, "Eli, Eli, lema sabachthani?" that is, "My God, my God, why have you forsaken me?" (Matthew 27:46). He was quoting Psalm 22, which was not only a cry from someone who was suffering, it was also a prophesy about his death and the deliverance it would bring.

The truth is, Jesus couldn't have sacrificed more to save us. He couldn't have traveled a greater distance to reach us. Thus, the cross was the greatest outpouring of love the world has ever known. The cross was the antithesis of sin. While sin creates a chronic inward focus that causes us to implode, the love shown on the cross is entirely self-sacrificial and outward facing. This is how Jesus destroyed the power of sin. His love displaced sin the same way that light displaces

BE FREE

darkness. Every human before him chose self-preservation, but Jesus demolished that cycle through his self-sacrifice. This was the one thing powerful enough to overcome sin. Martin Luther King Jr. understood this when he said, "Hate cannot drive out hate; only love can do that."

Though Jesus' death was part of the plan, it was not the final phase. Once Jesus destroyed sin, he turned his attention to eliminating death itself.

AIN'T NO GRAVE GONNA HOLD HIM DOWN

The Gospel writers recorded that two women went to visit Jesus' tomb after the crucifixion, but he wasn't there. Instead, they found an angel who claimed Jesus had risen and said they would see him in Galilee (Mark 16:6–7). Several days later, he was sitting on a beach eating breakfast with his disciples (John 21:12). In addition to repeatedly appearing to his friends, Jesus appeared to more than five hundred followers at the same time (1 Corinthians 15:6).

The power of the cross cannot be separated from the resurrection. It was by surrendering to death and then overcoming it that Jesus sealed the victory. The writer of Hebrews told us, "Since, therefore, the children share flesh and blood, he himself likewise shared the same things, so that through death he might destroy the one who has the power of death, that is, the devil…" (Hebrews 2:14). And the author of Second Timothy wrote, ". . . but it has now been revealed through the appearing of our Savior Christ Jesus, who abolished death and brought life and immortality to light through the gospel" (1:10).

Finally, Jesus explained to his friends that he had to leave again but promised he would be with them and reassured them that all authority in heaven and on earth had been given to him (Matthew 28:18). Then Jesus returned to the right hand of his Father, which is the position of authority (Mark 16:19).

THE LION WHO BECAME A LAMB

A LION, A LAMB, AND A WHITE HORSE

In the book of Revelation, John described a vision that conveys the reality of Jesus' triumph over the kingdom of darkness.

John saw a vision of a scroll that could not be opened. Some said it represented the future, which was sealed off from humanity.[4] Others believed it contained the secret of how God would defeat evil. At first, none were found worthy enough to open it. But then a lion appeared, the Lion of the tribe of Judah (Revelation 5:5). In the Old Testament, Jacob was speaking to his sons before he was about to die. To his son, Judah, he said, "your hand shall be on the neck of your enemies; your father's sons shall bow down before you. Judah is a lion's whelp . . ." (Genesis 49:8–9). The image of a lion speaks to the triumph over evil. And in his birth and life, we saw Jesus confronting evil with the strength of this lion.

But then the vision changed suddenly. It was like John blinked and the lion was gone. In his place was a lamb. But not just a lamb, the best description is "lambkin" or "poor little thing."[5] It was a small lamb, and what is more, the lamb had been fatally wounded (Revelation 5:6).

This lamb is a symbol of mercy. It feels like a polar contrast to the lion. The lamb is a common symbol throughout the Old Testament, almost always associated with sacrifice, specifically sacrifices made to deal with sin (Numbers 6:14). The lamb would die in the place of the guilty. When this image reappears in the New Testament, it is applied to Jesus. When John the Baptist saw Jesus walking toward him, he said, "Here is the Lamb of God who takes away the sin of the world!" (John 1:29).

So, which one is Jesus . . . the lion or the wounded lamb? The answer is both. Jesus is the lion who triumphed over everything that separated us from God. But he carried out this victory by becoming the lamb. He conquered death through dying.

Near the end of John's vision, the picture of Jesus changed again. John saw a rider on a white horse. He had fire in his eyes and many crowns on his head. He described this rider as a judge who rules with an iron rod. The rider also wore a robe stained with blood

BE FREE

(Revelation 19:11–16). Many have suggested the blood on the robe was that of his enemies, like a lion's mane made wet with the blood of a fresh kill. But if you read the entire chapter (and all of the preceding chapters) there is no previous battle described that involved Jesus in any sort of combat. He showed up on the battlefield with blood on his robe. The reason is simple. The rider is the lamb.[6] The blood on the robe of this rider did not belong to his enemies—the blood was his. The robe was stained because the lamb was slain. The cross and the resurrection cannot be separated. He endured death but then returned in victory and authority—riding on his horse.

HOW DOES THIS IMPACT US?

We can see the work Jesus did to overthrow the kingdom of darkness. But how is his victory transferred to us? How does the work he accomplished on a cosmic scale impact us on an individual level? In other words, how does his greater victory translate into our personal freedom from sin?

To answer these questions, we need to consider what we saw in Jesus' birth, life, death, resurrection, and ascension. Pay particular attention to the role of the Holy Spirit. Mary became pregnant with Jesus when the Holy Spirit overshadowed her (Luke 1:35). As Jesus grew, he increased in wisdom and divine favor (Luke 2:52). At his baptism, the Spirit descended on him like a dove (Matthew 3:16). He was led into the wilderness by the Spirit (Matthew 4:1) and he left the wilderness in the power of the Spirit (Luke 4:14). Jesus did what he saw his Father doing (John 5:19) and he drove out demons by the finger of God (Luke 11:20). Just before dying, Jesus said, "It is finished," and then he bowed his head and gave up his Spirit (John 19:30). Finally, Paul tells us that he was raised back to life by this same Spirit (Romans 8:11). Coming in human form, Jesus lived in dependence on the Father and lived by the power of the Holy Spirit.

The reason this is so important is because Paul went on in the same passage to say that the Spirit who raised Jesus from the dead dwells in us. This means Jesus' triumph over darkness can be applied to us. As humans, living by the power and work of the Holy Spirit, we can overcome Satan, sin, and death as Jesus did. Paul said our life can be hidden in Christ, and we participate with him in his death, resurrection, and ascension (Colossians 3:1–4).

We are caught up in the wave of his victory. This new reality is available to all of us, regardless of our past. Jesus was called the friend of tax collectors and sinners. He was also called a glutton and a drunkard (Matthew 11:19). He received these labels because of the company he kept. He was and is the friend of sinners. Jesus went to the places where sin was the thickest and worked there to distribute mercy.

John told us that God loves the world and that Jesus dealt with the sins of "the whole world" (John 3:16, 1 John 2:2). This freedom is available to anyone who wants it. None have fallen too far. This is how God responded to our sin—he disempowered it to set us free. Through Jesus the work is done. The prison door has been ripped off the hinges. So now there is just one question that remains—how will we respond?

CHAPTER 5

GIVING THE EULOGY AT MY OWN FUNERAL
DYING IN ORDER TO LIVE

TURN, THEN, AND LIVE

While the cross and resurrection was the culmination of God's plan to bring rescue and redemption to humanity, his mercy was evident all along. The prophets foretold of God's plan to destroy death and offer new life to all people.

Ezekiel wrote, "Have I any pleasure in the death of the wicked, says the Lord God, and not rather that they should turn from their ways and live?" (Ezekiel 18:23). Similarly, the prophet Isaiah said, "Seek the Lord while he may be found, call upon him while he is near; let the wicked forsake their way, and the unrighteous their thoughts; let them return to the Lord, that he may have mercy on them, and to our God, for he will abundantly pardon" (55:6–7).

It is clear, God does not wish for anyone to perish, and he is ready to abundantly pardon. The offer is there—open to anyone. But it is also important to see that a response is required. This mercy is extended to those who turn back to God. The verse from Ezekiel said, "Turn, then, and live." In other words, he has opened the door, now we need to stand up and walk out of prison.

In the book of Jonah, there is a powerful illustration of turning. God sent the prophet Jonah to the city of Nineveh to call out their wickedness (Jonah 1:1–3). Jonah ran at first, but God redirected him. Again, God instructed him to go to the city. Jonah obeyed and issued God's warning against them. The amazing part of this story is that the people of this city believed Jonah and repented. They chose to forfeit the violence of their hands, and God was merciful to them (Jonah 3:4–10). Because they were willing to turn, Nineveh became a city of rehabilitated criminals.

Interestingly, Jonah was upset. When he saw God's response to the turning of these people, he said, "That is why I fled . . . I knew that you are a gracious God and merciful, slow to anger, and abounding in steadfast love, and ready to relent from punishing" (Jonah 4:2). I am not sure why Jonah was upset other than that we sometimes seem to want mercy for ourselves and justice for others. Regardless, Jonah did summarize God's character well. He is slow to anger and abounding in steadfast love. This truth became even more visible in the New Testament.

In John's Gospel is a story about a woman who was caught committing adultery. The religious people in this story, like Jonah, wanted judgment against the woman. They were determined to kill her as was their custom. (Side note: I've often wondered what happened to the adulterous man, because he was guilty too.)

They brought the woman to Jesus and made her stand before all of them. I picture this woman encircled by a mob of angry men armed with stones. She probably feared to look up from the ground. The men demanded a response. At first, Jesus did not comply, but instead, he bent down to write something on the ground. I wonder if he was trying to catch the woman's eyes to remove her fear with the look of love on his face. When they continued to press him, he finally said, "Let anyone among you who is without sin be the first to throw a stone at her." When they heard this, the accusers began to leave one at a time—starting with the elders (John 8:1–9). The tension coursing through the woman must have drained from her body as the aggression dissipated and only the one who'd saved her remained.

I have always admired the brilliance of Jesus' response to the people in this story. However, I never realized how profound it was until recently. Jesus said anyone without sin could judge her. I thought there wasn't anyone there who was without sin. But I was wrong. There was one person present who had no sin—it was Jesus (2 Corinthians 5:21). He could have judged her. And yet, he didn't. Instead he saved her life and offered her mercy with the hope of rehabilitating her. After she realized no one was left to condemn her, Jesus said to the woman, "Neither do I condemn you. Go your way, and from now on do not sin again" (John 8:11). He showed mercy and then called her to turn.

Jesus makes it clear that the one condition to receive his mercy is that we turn back to God. We get to choose. It means that the only one who won't receive mercy is the one who doesn't want it (or doesn't think they need it).

TO THOSE WHO RECEIVE HIM

John called Jesus the light that shines in the darkness. He said the darkness could not overcome the light (John 1:5). It is possible to ignore the light and reject the truth Jesus offered. We can remain in our blindness, deceived about the severity of our condition. Some of those listening to Jesus talk about slavery tried to refute him. They said, "we are descendants of Abraham and have never been slaves to anyone" (John 8:33). They were still groping in the dark, unwilling to see their prison. They were in denial. This is the response John was referring to when he said, "He came to what was his own, and his own people did not accept him" (John 1:11).

As much as we can choose to shield ourselves from the light, we can also allow it to fall on us and remove the darkness we used to wear like a heavy coat. John went on to say, "But to all who received him . . . he gave power to become children of God . . ." (John 1:12).

This is a promise of restoration. John was telling us it is possible to recover what we lost at the Fall—our status as sons and daughters of God. Our relationship to our Father can be restored and therefore we can be free again. John said if we receive him, he will give us power. To receive Jesus is to turn and follow him (i.e. step out of prison). If we follow him, he will lead us back to the Father. We need to give up the thing that got us killed in the first place—our pursuit of independence. We need to be willing to return to dependence on God. To make this choice, we first need to acknowledge our sin and see what we've become. Otherwise, we won't see the need to step out and follow. The most common word to describe this process is confession.

BE FREE

CONFESSION

The restoration of our freedom starts with humility. We must confess and take ownership for our sin. We've all made choices that led us away from God and into the cycle of disordered attachment we discussed. Over time, our sin became normal, to the point that we lost our awareness of it. Rather than simply choosing it, we often neglect the choice to stop. But, still, we are accountable for our own sin.

In addition to being humble, we have to be fully honest. If we hold back and offer partial confessions to God, we will remain in prison. Sometimes we excuse or minimize certain sins. We don't want to call things what they are. God warned the people about treating their wounds as though they were not serious (Jeremiah 6:14). I once heard a teacher who compared this to the farmer who plants his crops but is unwilling to acknowledge the weeds and insects. We are reluctant to equate anger with murder and lust with adultery, but Jesus did, and we can't become free until we are willing to consider what he said. We need to acknowledge the reality and severity of our situation.

I am not referring only to the "bad stuff" I've done—the stuff that was obviously harmful. Remember that sin means to miss the mark. Our sin includes everything we became enslaved to in our search for independence. Lewis believed the basic sin behind all specific sins is the choice of self over God.[1] We need to take inventory of the things we have run to apart from God in our self-preservation and desperation to find life and fulfillment.

Some of the things we've chosen may be obvious, but some may not. As stated before, we are often not aware of all the attachments we've formed. The first thing we can do is ask God. David asked God to search him and find any hurtful or offensive way in him (Psalm 139: 23–24).

I am fully aware that I've struggled with anger, defensiveness, and lust at times in my life. But I've also looked to money for security, and to food (especially sugar) for comfort and joy. These are less obvious but still destructive.

Gerald May created a list of things people form attachments to based on feedback from his patients. In addition to things like anger, drinking, drugs, food, envy, lying, money, revenge, and sex, the list also included exercise, happiness, hobbies, relationships, the stock market, and sunbathing.[2]

These are not all bad things in and of themselves—some of them are very good. The danger is in our attachment to them. We've come to depend on these things in place of God, and this is the issue we need to acknowledge. Once we can acknowledge our sin and see how far we've run in the wrong direction, we are ready to decide to turn back to God. The other word for turning is repentance.

REPENTANCE (THE DECISION TO YIELD)

Jesus told a story about a son who demanded his inheritance while his father was still alive, and then left home. The son quickly squandered his money on empty pursuits and then found himself in a country ravaged by a famine. He took a job feeding pigs but was not offered any food; not even the pods reserved for the swine. Eventually, this son recognized what he'd done. He was literally starving and realized none of the things he'd consumed were able to fill him. It was from here he decided to return to his father (Luke 15:17–18).

Once we can see the things we've been clinging to for life, we need to start loosening our grip. Gerald May refers to this as detachment and describes it as a process of relinquishing.[3] This is where freedom begins. A. W. Tozer calls it the "blessedness of possessing nothing."[4]

We must release our hold on specific things, but it is also important to think of this on a larger scale. Ultimately, we have to let go of our pursuit of independence. The theologian Dietrich Bonhoeffer wrote, "Each man lives his own life, instead of all living the same God-life."[5] This is what has to change. We need to decide to trade our isolated life for a new God-life.

Jesus' friends once asked him how to pray. One of the first things he told them was to lay down their independence. He said, "Father, hallowed be your name, Your kingdom come" (Luke 11:2). To invite

BE FREE

God's kingdom means that we have to allow him to be king. I once heard Dallas Willard say that the greatest threat to the kingdom of God in our lives is our own kingdoms. If he is the king, we cannot be. Our job is to yield to him. And as we said before, this requires an act of trust.

We already dealt with hindrances to trusting God in chapter 3. We also read in chapter 4 that God gave everything to set us free, which means he is fully trustworthy. In light of this, there is certainly a willingness within me to choose to let go and yield to God. In my mind, I am on board and I can conceptualize this reality.

When I first began to think about the idea of detachment, I pictured myself standing on a hill in a strong wind. I was holding up a white sheet that was being used as a screen for a video projector. All of the objects of my attachment were displayed on the screen. Finally, I opened my hands and let go of the sheet. I watched as the wind ran off with my sins.

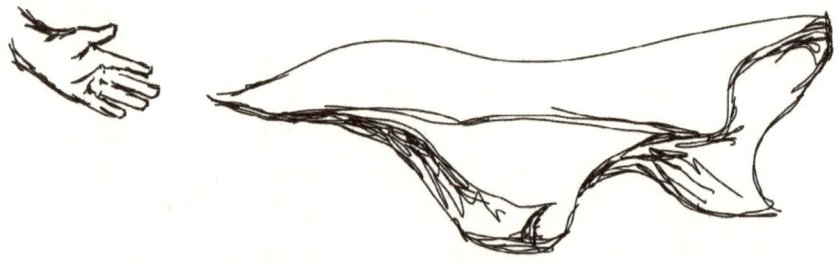

This was a good start. It was my way of grasping the idea of yielding my independence. Maybe you've done something similar where you made a mental decision to yield to God for the first time. This is an important mental shift. As we said, this whole thing starts with changing our thinking to align with the truth (i.e. reality). But it must go beyond this. We are talking about actually making him king. Deciding to let go and doing it are different. We have to take action and this is where things get difficult. While we may understand the need to yield, we don't really like to do it in practice.

My kids are all still rather young and prone to intense moments of rebellion. By rebellion I mean, body on the floor, thrashing, screaming, and kicking things over because we turned off the TV. Sometimes we will just let it go until they burn out. But other times I will pick them up, one arm under their knees and the other behind their shoulder. If a person were relaxed and calm, this would be a comfortable position—like sleeping in a hammock. But because they are moving and upset, I imagine it feels like sliding into a toilet bowl butt first. This is why I call it the "toilet bowl." I will hold them in this position until they stop fighting. The sooner they yield, the sooner Dad sets them down. They don't like it at all. None of us likes to yield because it means we have to give up control.

But more is going on here than just stubbornness. We are deciding to detach from things that have been there a long time. Even though Jesus has destroyed the power of sin, it still can feel like our sin runs deep. Many of us have formed strong attachments to things that seem to hold us like a tight rope around the wrists. As May said, this decision to follow Jesus is "alien territory" for many of us because we have chosen the "other" for so long.[6] It is more than just letting go. In reality, it can feel like consenting to surgery to have a limb removed. The truth is that we are being asked to die to our old selves.

TAKE UP YOUR CROSS

Jesus said that if we are going to follow him, we have to not only yield, but also take up a cross—as in the instrument of death (Matthew 16:24). The people who heard him say this knew more about crosses than we do. They were used to seeing bodies pinned to wooden poles alongside the road—a constant reminder from the Roman army that they were an occupied people. It was in this context that Jesus gave the instruction to pick up a cross. It is easy for us to spiritualize his words, but we need to realize that the decision to yield and follow can mean physical death. This has been the reality for many followers. But there is also a heart issue. The call of Jesus is to allow our old selves to be put to death.

BE FREE

You may be thinking this does not sound like the path to freedom. We are talking about yielding and dying. How does that lead to life? But here we must remember that our fight for independence only took us into prison. What we thought was life was actually death. We were already dead in our sin (Ephesians 2:1–5). When Jesus asks us to die, he is asking us to let go of something that is not good for us.

The choice to abandon our independence is a decision to stop looking to other things for life. We must reverse the decision we made in the garden. We must be willing to trade in everything we've known. This is a monumental act of surrender. But it is worth it because we get life. Willard refers to it as the "surrender of a lesser, dying self for a greater eternal one."[7] Jesus is asking us to die to the old self because he wants to resurrect the new self. He said, "those who lose their life for my sake, and for the sake of the gospel, will save it" (Mark 8:35). It is in losing our lives that we find life. If a grain of wheat falls to the earth and dies, it will bear fruit (John 12:24). In other words, the type of death Jesus invites us to is followed by a new birth.

BORN AGAIN

Children are born out of a struggle. I've witnessed my wife give birth five times. She is so beautiful and strong and she went through every labor with an uncommon grace. But with my hand on her back each time, there was no mistaking the pain pulsing through her body. One of the most amazing things about this is what happened to Heather (and to most mothers, I assume) after the kids were born. As soon as she had the baby in her arms, a calm rested on her shoulders like a light. She seemed to forget the pain almost instantly. There are few things as hopeful as birth. But what does it mean to be born again?

Jesus once told a man named Nicodemus that he had to be born again. Nicodemus couldn't understand what Jesus meant. He tried to envision how it would be possible for a grown man to climb back into the womb (John 3:1–21). Rebirth is a strange concept but the Gospel of Luke provides a series of stories that help explain what Jesus meant.

First, Luke told a story about a crowd of people around Jesus. They were bringing babies to Jesus for a blessing. Jesus' followers tried to intervene, but he prevented them, saying, "Let the little children come to me, and do not stop them; for it is to such as these that the kingdom of God belongs. Truly I tell you, whoever does not receive the kingdom of God as a little child will never enter it" (Luke 18:16–17). Remember, Jesus was surrounded by infants. He was telling us that if we want to find life in the kingdom, we have to become like babies. In the story that follows, he explained how.

A ruler asked Jesus about how to obtain eternal life. They talked about the good things the man had done and then Jesus identified the one thing the man was lacking. He told the man to sell everything he had and to give the money away. The man became sad because he was very wealthy (Luke 18:18–25). At first, this just sounds like a story about money, but it is actually a story about becoming a baby. I started to think about what would have happened if this man had followed Jesus' instructions. If he had literally sold everything, he would have been left with nothing—not even clothing.

Heather and I saw a man like this once when we were first married. One night we woke up to a loud sound outside our Fargo, ND apartment complex. We pulled apart the blinds and looked out our window. There was a man standing outside a ground-level apartment in the building across from us. He was pounding on the sliding glass door and yelling. Then, unexpectedly, the man took off his shirt and pulled down his pants to his ankles. As the naked man stood there in the snow waving his arms, I finally realized what he was saying. His message to the person on the other side of the glass was, "I have nothing!"

If the rich ruler had obeyed Jesus, he would have been in the same place as the man in Fargo. He would have been left wandering along the side of the road, naked and helpless. I can imagine him muttering to himself, "I have nothing." This man would have needed to fully depend on someone else to meet his needs. And in that sense, he would have been just like a baby.

I don't necessarily think Jesus was asking the man to lose his clothes. But he was asking the ruler to let go of his attachments. He was asking him to discontinue his dependence on everything he had acquired so he could depend on God—like a baby depends on his or her parents.

And now the connection becomes clear. The decision to die and the decision to be born again are the same decision. In the same moment that we die to the old self, we are born to God. The practice that confirms this inward transformation is called baptism.

BAPTISM

From the outside, baptism looks like dunking people under the water. And in one sense, that is all it is. It is not magic. But in another sense, it is much more. It is the expression of something profound.

A baptism is actually a funeral. The act of going under the water is the burial of the old self. But it is a strange funeral because the one being baptized actually delivers the eulogy (some call it a testimony). In baptism, we confess our dead condition and declare our need for God. Then we die. But it is okay because our death is followed by an immediate birth. At one point, Paul said we are crucified with Christ and another time he said we are buried with him in baptism (Galatians 2:19, Colossians 2:12). But he also said the Spirit that raised Jesus lives in us and restores our life (Romans 8:11). Our crucifixion and burial are followed by resurrection.

This resurrection is initiated by God's Spirit entering into us. Before leaving, Jesus promised his disciples that they would receive power from the Holy Spirit. Then a short time later, the Spirit fell on them at Pentecost (Acts 1:8, 2:1–4). Actually, this help had been promised long before the invasion (Incarnation). The prophet Ezekiel wrote, "A new heart I will give you, a new spirit I will put within you . . ." (36:26).

I was first baptized as a baby. I will always be deeply grateful for a family who committed me to God before I could even comprehend him. It was a sign that they trusted God and our church with my future.

However, as I grew up, I pursued the self-rule and independence we've been talking about. I had not made the decision to die to myself. Then one weekend, I went camping with some coworkers

GIVING THE EULOGY AT MY OWN FUNERAL

(a group that included my future wife). We were attending an outdoor concert series. On the first day, we learned of a man who was going to preach a sermon down by the lake. He was a prison chaplain (ironically) with spiked hair and a healthy beard. He talked about sin and about yielding to God. Then he invited any who were willing to join him in the lake to be drowned. A line of people followed the preacher into the water like a tail swishing in the shallows. I joined them. Heather took the photograph shown below. It is my second baby picture.

At our new birth, we are declaring ourselves dead to sin. It is our act of turning and receiving the mercy he offers us. It is our definitive choice to step out of prison and be restored to our status as the children of God. Life and death are literally in front of us and God wants us to choose life (Deuteronomy 30:19). This is never a decision we could have made on our own. Everything written in previous chapters is confirmation of that. But thankfully, through the work of Jesus and the power of the Holy Spirit, our choice has been restored and a way has been made for us to return. We can now see the need to die to the old self in order to receive new life. Through this decision, we are transferred from the kingdom of darkness into the kingdom of God's son (Colossians 1:13). This is powerful and beautiful. It sounds like a great ending to a story. However, this is not the end of our story—it is just the beginning.

BE FREE

ONE CHOICE FOLLOWED BY A MILLION MORE

Once we step into freedom, we need to learn how to walk in it. Paul said we must learn to walk by the Spirit (Galatians 5:16). It starts with one choice, but it involves a million more over the course of our lives with God. Paul also said that he needed to die every day (1 Corinthians 15:31). This is a process that we enter into with God. Think of a child growing up under the care, protection, and instruction of his or her parents.

Our freedom is already a reality but our experience of it is a process that can only happen in relationship with God through the Holy Spirit. We are already free but we have to learn to live this way. The cells in a newborn baby already contain the DNA needed to construct a full-grown adult. But growing up is a process. And it is a process that requires dependence. A baby left to itself will simply not survive.

It is also important to remember that our new birth is actually a rebirth. We have this other life we lived, possibly for a long time. So our growing process actually involves retraining and rehabilitation. God wants to rehabilitate us so we do not just return to the former ways. We broke covenant the first time. If we go unchanged, we will inevitably drift toward independence again. We are not only branches plucked out of the fire (Zechariah 3:2) but branches that have been grafted back onto the vine, and he wants us to remain there to receive his life (John 15:5).

Finally, we need to recognize that there is still a force that exists who stands opposed to our freedom. We know Satan still exists because Peter told us to keep alert (1 Peter 5:8) and Paul told us to put on armor to defend against the flaming arrows of the evil one (Ephesians 6:11). Because Satan still exists, there is still a battle. But as author and teacher Graham Cooke explained, it's not a fair fight. Before he went to the cross, Jesus said the ruler of this world would be driven out (John 12:31). Satan is on the run, and any remnant of power he still has is dwarfed by the power of God. What's more, we know that God's power is available to us. My daughter once said, referring to the devil, "God took away his bucket of weapons and gave them to us." That was her translation of Colossians 2:15, which says he has been disarmed. John said the one who is in us is greater than the one who is in the world (1 John 4:4). And all the way back in Genesis, God promised he would strike the head of the serpent, which means we can, too, because his Spirit is in us (Genesis 3:15). We have power over the evil one because when Jesus returned to the Father and took his position of authority, he shared it with us. He made us alive again, raised us up and seated us with him in heavenly places in Christ Jesus (Ephesians 2:5–6). We don't have to fear Satan.

Having said that, there is one skill the devil has retained—his ability to deceive. This is because deceit is the essence of his nature (John 8:44). If he is still alive, he can still lie to us. He will use condemnation (to shame us into thinking we haven't changed), temptation (to draw us away from God again), and intimidation (to make us think God has abandoned us). He uses these lies to undermine our relationship with God and lead us back into prison. These lies are all aimed at isolating us.

The good news is he can only influence us if he deceives us into believing he has power. The wizard had a large amount of power over people in Oz. Not because he was strong, but because he convinced people that he was. That is why the lion jumped through a window at the sound of his amplified voice. It seemed real, but it was all smoke and mirrors. In other words, Satan can't gain power over us unless we let him. It is only when we don't acknowledge him or when we try to fight him on our own that we are in danger. If we stay alert and stay close to Jesus, we will overcome. In that spirit, it is time to look at the first tactic of the enemy, which is condemnation.

CHAPTER 6

A WATER BOTTLE FOR ASTRONAUTS
ESCAPING CONDEMNATION

FORGIVEN AND REDEEMED

We looked extensively at how Jesus came to rescue and restore us. Paul said, "In him we have redemption through his blood, the forgiveness of our trespasses, according to the riches of his grace" (Ephesians 1:7). Though we ran from God, he pursued us. Though we rejected God, he still accepts us. And though we were hostile toward God, he gave his life to save us. That is forgiveness. But remember, he also wants to change us. God wants to rehabilitate us and keep us out of prison. He wants to restore us into what we were intended to be. That is redemption. We need to understand both to experience freedom.

For a long time, I only knew half the story. I knew about sin and forgiveness, but I had no concept of redemption. This kept me from walking in freedom. To illustrate what I mean, I need to tell you about a river.

THE DIRTIEST RIVER ON EARTH

I once saw a picture of two boys swimming in a river. They were floating on their backs and only their faces and hands were visible. One boy had a plastic bag across his chest like a life jacket. Garbage was all around them. They both had their eyes closed and their lips sealed. Gray water dripped from their hair.

The boys were swimming in the Citarum River in Indonesia. Many believe this is one of the most polluted rivers on earth. Over five hundred factories line the banks of the river, and in most places, you can't see the water because the garbage floating on the surface is so dense. It looks like it could be an alley instead of a river, and it is more profitable to forage for trash than to fish it.[1]

This is a good picture of the human soul apart from God. This is what sin does to us. All the things we try to fill ourselves with will end up choking the life out of us. As long as I can remember, I have been aware of this reality. I always had an understanding that I was polluted because of sin. At the same time, I knew about forgiveness. I knew that God saw the dirty condition of my soul and still loved me in spite of it. While this is good news, it is incomplete. I had no concept of redemption, and so I was unaware that God could actually change me. As a result, I believed that though God accepted me, I was still the same old person. Nothing about me was fundamentally different. I still looked the same on the inside. The biggest problem with thinking this way is it kept me from changing; it kept me trapped in the same sins. The truth is, we always act on what we believe. Remember, the heart directs the mind and the mind directs the body. If I believe the truest thing about me is that I am a dirty sinner with no hope of ever changing, I probably won't change.

Think back to the river for a moment. Imagine you are walking along the Citarum River eating a granola bar. What would you do with the wrapper once you were done? I am not someone who litters, but to be honest, it would not be hard to throw a wrapper into that river. It looks like a garbage dump, so it wouldn't feel much different from throwing a wrapper into a wastebasket. It is the same with us. If I believe I am still polluted, my actions will confirm it.

Because I had no sense of redemption, I remained trapped in my sin, which led me into a downward spiral of shame. Eventually, the shame gave way to condemnation.

THE CYCLE OF SHAME

My tangible experience of Christianity often felt like a cycle. I would fall to sin and then feel bad about what I'd done. In my despair, I would repent and seek forgiveness. Then I would resolve not to do that thing anymore. This would last for a little while until I sinned again. It felt like each time around, the bad feelings got worse.

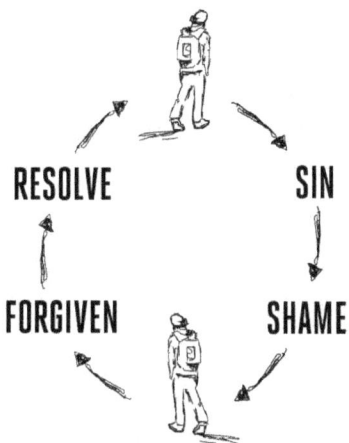

When I was in middle school, I learned to play the guitar, and eventually I started writing music. A while back, I was looking over the words to some of the songs I'd written. Almost every song was about the feeling of spinning down a drain. I confessed my sin through lyrics and pleaded for forgiveness. Then did it again a few days later. In one of the songs, I did write about freedom, but it was a distant idea—like a tiny dot rocking on the ocean at the edge of the horizon. I must have had some sense that freedom was the point, but it was blurry and abstract. The only tangible thing was my repeated sin. Looking back, it seems I only identified myself by my sin.

When you live with the awareness that something is wrong, and you can't seem to get free of it, it is hard to avoid being overcome with a sense of failure that eventually gives way to shame. And the problem with shame is that it causes us to isolate ourselves. We don't want others to see our filth, so we hide—even from God (Genesis 3).

The longer I struggled with the same sins, the more my shame piled up. The more shame, the more I wanted to hide. This caused me to distance myself further and further from God. I had this sense that God would eventually grow weary of me. I knew he still accepted me but I feared there would be a limit to the number of

BE FREE

times I could come back seeking forgiveness (now I know this is a lie, but I didn't at the time).

Of course, the more I distanced myself from God, the more susceptible I was to sin. This brought on more shame and down I went. Eventually, I reached a point where I felt completely hopeless that anything would ever change. I believed I was fated to live forever in this destructive cycle. In other words, I lived under condemnation. Thankfully, I didn't stay there.

NO CONDEMNATION

Paul wrote, "There is therefore now no condemnation for those who are in Christ Jesus" (Romans 8:1). This reminds me of what Jesus said to the adulteress woman mentioned earlier from John 8. After silencing the hypocrites, he said those beautiful words, "Neither do I condemn you" (John 8:11). The reoccurring theme throughout the New Testament is that anyone who has yielded to Jesus is free of condemnation.

As I began to understand this, it led to an important question. If God wasn't condemning me, who was? It was in seeking the answer to this question that I first began to learn that I had an enemy.

John identified Satan as the "accuser of our comrades [or brothers]" and stated that he accuses God's people day and night (Revelation 12:10). To accuse someone is to bring a charge against them. An accuser lays out your past before you and broadcasts your guilt. If you listen to accusations, you will have a hard time escaping your past. And if I am defined by my broken past, I will likely feel shame and an inability to change—exactly the trap I was describing before. It was the deception of the accuser that brought me under condemnation and kept me from experiencing freedom. Realizing that was vital for me, but then I had to do something about it.

Let me say this again, to overcome deception, we simply need to take hold of the truth. In fact, this is exactly what John said to do with the accuser. He wrote, "But they have conquered him [the accuser] by the blood of the Lamb and the word of their testimony . . ."

A WATER BOTTLE FOR ASTRONAUTS

(Revelation 12:11). What is a testimony? It is a declaration of the truth from someone who has witnessed it. The truth that we must declare in order to combat condemnation is redemption. Because of the blood of the Lamb, we've not only been forgiven, but redeemed. To understand what it means to be redeemed, we need to look at the idea of restoration.

RESTORATION

The more I thought about the Citarum River and the image of the boys floating in that garbage, the more I began to sense the Holy Spirit trying to speak to me. Finally, I realized something that changed my life: the river hadn't always looked that way. There had been a time when the water rolling through that trench was pure and undefiled. There was a time when you could have pressed your face into that river and taken a drink without the risk of bacteria infiltrating your body. The impurities had been added; they had been acquired over time. If the impurities were added, it stands to reason that they could be taken away. And if impurities could be removed, it was possible for the water to be restored.

I did some research on water filtration to see if there was any hope for restoring the Citarum River. First, I came across a video on YouTube advertising a water bottle with a built-in filtration system. The makers stated they'd used NASA technology to design the water filter that is contained within the lid.

BE FREE

The video demonstrated the power of this filter by filling the bottle with Coke, securing the lid, and then squeezing out the contents into a glass. The liquid that came out of the water bottle was clean and clear, like pure water.

While this is impressive, purifying a bottle of water is not the same as restoring an entire river. As I continued my research, I came across another story that filled me with hope. I found an article about the River Thames that flows through London. I learned that fifty years ago, this river was considered biologically dead, and people regularly contracted sickness from the water. [2] But then the article explained that the government had launched an ambitious restoration effort that involved stronger regulation for factories and the construction of water treatment plants all along the river. The amazing part of the story is that the River Thames is now considered to be one of the cleanest rivers that flows through a major city on earth.

The takeaway is clear—with a strong enough filter, dirty things can be restored. This is going to sound strange, but the more I learned about the water filtration system, the more I imagined applying it to our human nature. I envisioned God picking me up and turning me upside down over his hand. Filthy water poured out of me and ran through his fingers. The clean water, dripping from the bottom of his hand, collected in a large, wooden bowl.

This is not just wishful thinking. John wrote, "If we confess our sins, he who is faithful and just will forgive us our sins and cleanse us from all unrighteousness" (1 John 1:9). When God cleanses us from our unrighteousness, our unrighteousness (or sin) is removed. If our sin can be removed, it means something about us has fundamentally changed. We are not the same. Like the river, the sin and brokenness we acquired can be removed.

HE TAKES AWAY OUR SIN

The psalmist wrote, ". . . as far as the east is from the west, so far he removes our transgressions from us" (Psalm 103:12). How far is east from west? If you get in the car and start heading west, you will never find east. And the prophet Zechariah wrote,

> Then he showed me the high priest Joshua standing before the angel of the LORD, and Satan standing at his right hand to accuse him. And the LORD said to Satan, "The LORD rebuke you, O Satan! The LORD who has chosen Jerusalem rebuke you! Is not this man a brand plucked from the fire?" Now Joshua was dressed with filthy clothes as he stood before the angel. The angel said to those who were standing before him, "Take off his filthy clothes." And to him he said, "See, I have taken your guilt away from you, and I will clothe you with festal apparel." —Zechariah 3:1–4

The removing of the filthy clothes symbolized the taking away of sin. It was and is an act of restoration. And notice that God didn't just redeem Joshua, but he also defended him from the accuser; further evidence that there is no condemnation for the redeemed.

Recall the story of the angel who told Mary to call her son Jesus because he would save his people from sin (Matthew 1:21). And once Jesus was fully grown, his cousin John identified him as "the Lamb of God who takes away the sin of the world" (John 1:29). Remember the Revelation passage that tells us we overcame the enemy by the blood of this Lamb (Revelation 12:11).

Once I began to understand redemption, I realized that it is everywhere in the Bible.

EVERYTHING HAS BECOME NEW

There is a beautiful statement in Isaiah chapter 61. It comes right after the proclamation Jesus read about liberating captives and binding up the brokenhearted. Through Isaiah, God said to those who mourn, I will give them "a garland instead of ashes, the oil of gladness instead of

BE FREE

mourning, the mantle of praise instead of a faint spirit" (Isaiah 61:3).

Author and teacher Graham Cooke points out that the most powerful word in this passage is the word *instead*. God is promising to remove the old and replace it with the new. Dallas Willard used to say that God's intention is not to help us deal with sin, it is to turn us into the kind of people who don't want to sin anymore. The idea here is transformation.

My boys have a fascination with war history. I love their courage but have been trying to teach them that our battle is not against flesh and that people are not our enemies. I tell them that the best way to win a war is not to kill the bad guys. It is to turn the bad guys into good guys.

I heard a story about a man who was part of a militant group that was strongly opposed to Christianity. This man was personally responsible for the deaths of many Christians. But then he began to have this dream where he was looking down at his hands and they were stained red. No matter how hard he tried, the man could not clean his hands. Eventually, the dreams turned into visions that happened while he was awake, and he believed he was going crazy. But then one day, the vision changed. As he was trying to clean his hands, a man in white came to him and told him that he could make him clean. From that day on, the man who had once killed Christians risked his life to tell other people about the man in white.

Isaiah said that though we were stained red, we would be made white as snow (Isaiah 1:18). Have you noticed how dreary things look in a mild winter? Everything dies, the grass loses all color, and that muddy paste covers the streets and sprays the world every time a car passes by. But sometimes the air slows down enough and a fresh snow falls. The pieces are small and make no sound when they hit the earth, but after a while, they accumulate into a mass that covers the ground. Everything becomes white. When the sunlight hits the ground, you have to squint. Everything looks pure and new.

If you have trouble relating to the precipitation imagery, consider the analogy of a child. John said we have been made into children of God (1 John 3:2). Try to envision a robe of woven fabric being draped around your shoulders. Imagine the feeling of a heavy ring made of rare metal twisting onto your finger. And hear the Father yelling about throwing a party because his son or daughter who was lost has been found (Luke 15).

And the metaphors keep getting better. I was praying about this idea of newness, and I saw an image of my wife in her wedding dress. The sun was setting and its fading light was leaking through small gaps in the trees. A hundred tiny spotlights highlighted her shoulders. She was standing under the branch of a tree in bloom. The wind breathed on the branch and caused the blossoms to vibrate and then tear free from the buds. White petals were floating, but not falling—as though they were suspended in midair. She looked like a painting, but it was a living painting because the light kept changing and the breeze pulled pieces of hair across her cheek. Paul compared the church to a bride and said that Christ not only gave himself up for her, but that he cleanses her with the washing of water (Ephesians 5:25–27).

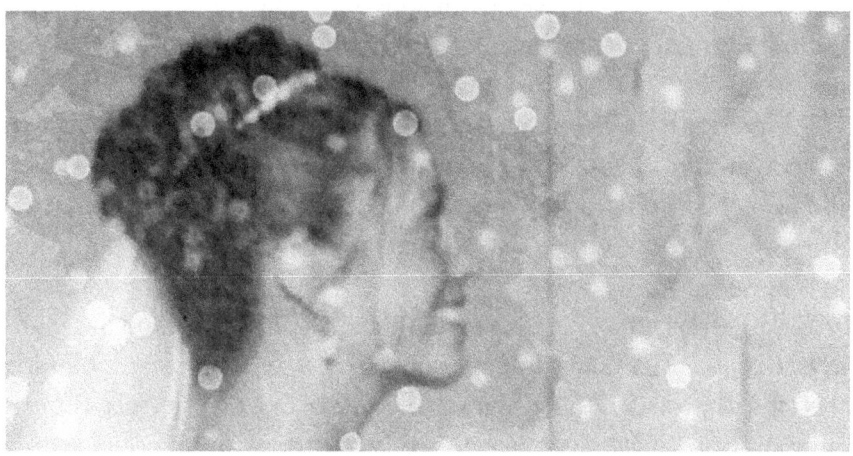

Peter went even further when he wrote, "But you are a chosen race, a royal priesthood, a holy nation, God's own people, in order that you may proclaim the mighty acts of him who called you out of darkness into his marvelous light" (1 Peter 2:9). God actually calls us holy.

Finally, the Bible moves beyond familiar imagery to proclaim that God is inviting us into something entirely new. "So if anyone is in Christ, there is a new creation: everything old has passed away; see,

BE FREE

everything has become new!" (2 Corinthians 5:17). Paul said that God calls things into existence that did not exist (Romans 4:17) and Ezekiel prophesied, "A new heart I will give you, and a new spirit I will put within you; and I will remove from your body the heart of stone and give you a heart of flesh" (Ezekiel 36:26).

This is our reality; it is the resurrected condition of our souls. This is what we look like because of the restorative power of Jesus. We are clean as the winter, and we are his sons and daughters. We are a bride and a holy nation. We have entered a new reality where freedom is within reach.

We truly have been given a new nature. Now the task is to learn to grow into it. We have to make a choice to "clothe" ourselves with the new self (Ephesians 4:24). We need to begin to believe the truth of our restoration. Greg Boyd wrote, "We are transformed according to that on which we fix our minds."[3]

If we can start to see ourselves in the new reality that God has made available, we can begin to experience freedom. If we can abandon the view that we are filled with trash and see our own souls as pure, running water, we will be far less likely to keep polluting ourselves.

Embracing our new identity is vital, but condemnation is not the only tactic of the enemy. If he cannot keep us under the shame of our past, he will try to distract us from moving forward. He does this through temptation.

CHAPTER 7

MADE OUT OF PLASTIC
OVERCOMING TEMPTATION

There are two things I remember about driving in the car with my dad when I was growing up. One is that the car often smelled like a lawn mower, which is not a bad thing. The other thing is that he always listened to oldies. While I can't recall any complete songs, I do remember short segments of songs. There are all these little sound bites floating around in my head that surface occasionally. One of the most familiar is a line from a song called "Oh, Boy!" performed by Buddy Holly. The opening line to the song was, "All of my love, all of my kissin', you don't know what you've been missin', oh boy!"

While not intended this way, this song is actually a good paraphrase of the first temptation that took place back in the garden. Remember what the serpent offered Adam and Eve—he said if they ate they would be like God. The people heard this and thought the tree was a delight to the eyes and so they ate. The other key thing to pull from the story was the false reassurance the serpent offered when he told Eve, "You will not die" (Genesis 3:4).

The tactic of the serpent was simple; he got Adam and Eve to believe they were missing out on something better than what they had. His goal, as we saw, was to draw them away from God by getting them to search for life somewhere else. Specifically, the enemy did two things to accomplish this—we could call these the anatomy of temptation...

First, he tapped into desire. The serpent drew their attention to something that was a delight to the eyes and was to be desired to make one wise. He was presenting them with alternatives that seemed good.

Second, the serpent tried to get the couple to overlook the natural consequences of following their desire by convincing them there would be no negative results. Thus he was able to get them to fall more easily.

BE FREE

Just like in the garden, the enemy uses temptation to pull us away from life with God and lead us back into prison. Pastor Kris Vallotton compares Satan's strategy to the algorithms used in on-line direct marketing. The marketers know where we've been in the past and will send us specific ads based on those patterns; trying to show us what we are missing and prompting us to come back.

When we are confronted with the temptation to return to our old sins, the subtle voice of the enemy aims to highlight the perceived benefits while negating the true consequences. This is, of course, a deception. The moment we pursue the option being presented to us, the false promise of Satan is exposed. One of the writers of proverbs stated the prospect of adultery appeared smoother than oil but left the impact of a sharp, two-edged sword (Proverbs 5:3–4).

Temptation is something that everyone faces. The first step in facing temptation is to recognize that it is not the same as sin.

HOW SIN IS BORN

The book of James describes temptation as a process. It says we are first tempted when something taps into our desires. If we are lured by the desire and stay with it long enough, it can conceive and give birth to sin. When the sin is fully grown, it gives birth to death (James 1:14–15). James ends by admonishing us not to be deceived (James 1:16).

It all starts as a deception. If it is possible for us to avoid being deceived, it means we have the choice to go the right way. Remember, we are dead to sin, our nature has been changed, and we've been given a new heart (Ezekiel 36:26). We don't have to sin. It is only if we choose to follow the deception that sin is conceived and born. In other words, there is a specific point in the process where temptation takes us into sin. Before it reaches that point, we have the opportunity to make a decision that will determine a better outcome.

Not only does this mean we can overcome temptation, it means temptation is not the same thing as sin. Remember, Jesus was tempted and yet did not sin (Hebrews 4:15). This is vital to understand because if we think they are the same, we will believe we are guilty of sin every time we experience temptation. And because temptation comes at us from an outside source that is calling to our old desires, it is often beyond our control when we are tempted. If I am guilty every time this happens, then I will have trouble feeling like I'm making any progress and will likely end up back under condemnation.

It is good news that temptation and sin are different. It is also good news that we don't have to be deceived into choosing sin because we have been changed by the work of Jesus. Having said that, it is also true that temptation can be overwhelming and there are times when we will feel like we really do want to go back to what we've been "missin'." So why does it feel so hard? One reason it feels hard is because all the things we used to look to for life are still within our reach. We still live in the same environment we did before choosing to follow Jesus into freedom. The Bible refers to this environment as "the World."

THE WORLD

We can think of the world as a collective or a system. It is not a single thing, but the compilation of everything that exists in physical reality. The world is not inherently evil—God made it and everything in it (including us). Unfortunately, the world system has been corrupted. John said, "the whole world lies under the power of the evil one" (1 John 5:19).

People all around us are being assaulted by deception, just as we are. The cumulative effect of this is a system that supports independence from God. Pornography, materialism, the corruption of power, the drug culture, violence, etc. are all part of the system we live in. No one person is responsible for these things, but we've all been influenced by the enemy and contributed in some way to creating a monster that has grown far beyond our control and now rolls over everything in its path. Paul called this phenomenon the patterns of this world (Romans 12:2).

We've contributed, but we also suffer from it. Even as we are seeking to get free from sin, we can and will be impacted by other people's sin.

BE FREE

The world can continue to wound us and then our brokenness can lead us back to searching for comfort and relief in places apart from God.

As we saw before, we may be changing, but the system is still here impacting us. The temptation to sin and the feelings of brokenness can seem even more prevalent and obvious to us now because there is a discrepancy between our new hearts and everything around us. When we were unaware of our deception, we just followed the course of this world (Ephesians 2:2). But now we are going the other way. Imagine walking in a crowded airport in the same direction of traffic and then suddenly turning and attempting to walk the opposite way. We would instantly become far more aware of the people around us, and they would also begin running into us.

The options to find life apart from God are almost infinite, and now they are very noticeable. It may feel hard to direct our attention away from them. In other words, our old life is right there to remind us, and our old desires can be activated. It is true, fundamental changes are taking place within us. Having said that, we still live in bodies that are in the process of being restored. The pull that we still feel is because of old habits that exist in our bodies. The good news is that habits can be broken.

THE FLESH

Like the world, our bodies are not inherently evil. God made our bodies and called them good (Genesis 1:31). Willard reminds us of the simple idea that humans had physical bodies before the Fall, which means our bodies once functioned apart from sin.[1]

The problem is that our bodies became corrupted just like the world. Sin gained control over our mortal bodies (Romans 6:13). The Bible often refers to the fallen state of the human body as "the flesh." We've looked at our struggle with the flesh in terms of our attachments and addictions. We also explored how Jesus freed us from our bodies of sin and death (Romans 7:24–25). These words are hopeful, but sometimes don't fit with our experience. The old patterns and habits and attachments still feel very real, even after we've made the decision to die to those things. It can be discouraging, but there is an explanation for this.

The restoration of the physical body is a process. Paul said that the reality of Jesus' Spirit dwelling in us "will give life to [our] mortal bodies" (Romans 8:11). Jesus has freed our bodies, but he is also bringing life to our bodies through his Spirit. The victory is won but the work is still taking place.

Our bodies are plastic in the sense that they are pliable or shapeable. Author William James explained, "Plasticity means the possession of a structure weak enough to yield to an influence, but strong enough not to yield all at once . . . [and] the phenomena of habit in living beings are due to [this] plasticity."[2] In other words, our bodies can be shaped and transformed over time. This is how sin got such a strong hold on us in the first place (remember the descent into prison in chapter 2). Thankfully, it also means we can be reshaped or transformed back into what we were meant to be. This good transformation, or restoration, can also take time.

The longer we struggle with something, the stronger the attachment becomes. According to May, "In prolonged addictions, what may initially have involved a rather simple change in a few million synapses has progressively expanded to affect billions of cells . . ."[3]

BE FREE

I've struggled with an attachment to sugar for over thirty years. I remember once stealing cookies as a kid. I didn't take one; I took the whole container into the bathroom and hid. When I was in high school, Krispy Kreme Doughnuts came to our city. My friends and I celebrated by each buying a dozen donuts and eating them in one sitting. Then we made homemade T-shirts with the logo on the front. Years later, when I worked in a cubical, one of the ladies who worked on my team had a passion for baking. Once she brought in four kinds of wedding cake for us to sample. I took a large piece of each. My over-desire for sugar has often felt like a beast inside me, and I fed it for most of my life. That is why the hold feels so strong even though I know I can be free of it.

May also talks about what he calls "addiction memory" in the cells. He says that when we are exposed to the old sources of attachment, it can "fire up old cell patterns once again."[4] We are dead to sin, but now we must enter the process of reprogramming and coming back alive to God.

Think of a train moving at high speed. Once it's going, it is easy for it to keep moving in the same direction. However, if that train needs to stop and change directions, an immense amount of force is required. Even once the brakes are applied, a fast train needs extensive lengths of track to stop. It will also require energy to move in the new direction. Jesus stopped the train when he defeated sin and death. Now power is needed to start in a new direction. The Holy Spirit is meant to be the primary source of this power, but the Bible indicates that we also need to take an active role in the process. In other words, our participation is required.

OUR REHABILITATION

Paul instructed us not to offer our members to sin as instruments of wickedness, but to offer our members to God as instruments of righteousness (Romans 6:13). Therefore, we must choose to retrain our bodies. This is why I said before that the choice to follow Jesus is not passive. In our areas of sin and addiction, our hearts went to sleep and we stopped actively choosing. The heart has to wake up, and we need to begin exercising our will again. He restored our ability to choose God—now we must use it.

We have an active role and our will is involved. But we are meant to engage in this process with the constant partnership of God through the Holy Spirit. He is the one who can restore life to our mortal bodies, and our job is to cooperate. Think of it as though the Holy Spirit is a physical therapist that is going to help us learn to walk again after a severe injury. Jesus said the Holy Spirit would teach us everything (John 14:26). While this is good news, it also presents us with a problem.

This rehabilitation process is not taking place in a large, open room with peaceful music and light pouring in through giant windows. Our rehabilitation is taking place on a battlefield. Our retraining process is happening while we are actively under attack and the hiss of bullets cutting through the air can be heard on all sides. The temptations around us don't get put on hold for a few months so we can finish our program first. The two are happening simultaneously.

A fair question to ask at this point would be why? Why doesn't God take us out of combat for a season so we can get better first? Or . . . why doesn't he just zap us to make us better and then we would be ready to slap away any temptation that flies at us?

The reason we still face temptation while we are a work in progress is because temptation is an inherent part of freedom. We said before that Jesus restored our choice when he set us free. If it is true that we have the ability to make genuine choices, then there will always be options. To be able to choose is to have the option to go left or right—to walk with God or walk alone again. The only way to remove all temptation would be to remove our choice, which would destroy our freedom.

Why doesn't God just fix us rather than taking us through a process? Because without the training process, we would fall right back into sin. We broke covenant with God the first time. Without going through a process that brings about our transformation, what is to say we would not just break it again? Jesus rescued us when we weren't even looking to be rescued. But the redemption is something we have to sign up for.

It is available, and he wants to change us, but it just doesn't happen without a partnership and a process.

In future chapters we will look at some practical ways to engage with God through the Holy Spirit to participate in the process of our redemption. We are going to learn how to live in the freedom he's given us. But because we are actively under temptation the entire time we are trying to engage that process, I want to offer a few practical tactics for facing temptation before we move on.

TACTICS AGAINST TEMPTATION

In our moments of fierce, and perhaps unexpected, temptation or testing, there are several things we can do to stay free:

Find the Exit and Run

No matter how hard the temptation feels, we need to remember that God always provides a way out (1 Corinthians 10:13). During temptation, I ask God out loud to show me the way out. Then I make a run for it. There are two reasons this is helpful. First, by saying God's name out loud, I am forcing myself to remember that he is there with me. If I trick myself into to thinking I'm alone, it is much harder to overcome. Second, the longer we stand on the edge, the more likely we are to fall. Proverbs says to free yourself like a gazelle from the hunter or like a bird from a fowler (Proverbs 6:5). I am not an animal expert, but I do know gazelles run and birds fly. It is not being a coward, it is being wise.

One of the largest areas of struggle facing humanity is the abuse of our sexuality. The assault is everywhere, so the chances of being ambushed are high. Unless we live alone in a cave (which I don't recommend) we will encounter sexual temptation often—probably daily. This is why Paul gave the instruction to flee from (or in some translations, to shun) sexual sin (1 Corinthians 6:18, 2 Timothy 2:22). It reminds me of Joseph in the Old Testament. He worked for an officer of Pharaoh named Potiphar. Potiphar's wife began to make sexual advances toward him. At one point, she grabbed his clothes and tried to seduce him. Joseph turned and fled. He was so intent on running that he left his garment behind (Genesis 39:12). Better to lose my shirt than my freedom.

Be Real
The next thing to do in the heat of temptation is to be real about the consequences of the action. Remember, the enemy wants to downplay this. And unless we make a definitive choice to think about the consequences, it is easy to choose ignorance. Remember James showed us the process of temptation. It starts by tapping into our inside world before any action takes place. If I feel a desire to sin rising up in me, I will try to have a quick conversation with myself that goes something like this: "If I decide to go through with this, it will feel great for a few minutes or maybe an hour. Then reality will set in, and I will feel regret for pursuing something that leads to death. The wine always ends up turning to poison in my stomach. Also, if I go through with this, it will be that much harder to resist the next time."

While this is helpful, it is even more helpful to focus on the positive of what will happen if I walk away. I may say, "I know that in the past, the choice to walk away from this has led to immense joy. If I avoid this deception, I know I will wake up feeling relieved and peaceful because I made the right choice. I also know I will be stronger the next time this thing calls to me." The idea is simply replacing the deception with the truth. It is aligning our minds with the Spirit of truth—even if that means talking to ourselves.

Resist Just Once
A while back, I noticed a pattern of self-deception that I'd fallen into. I had convinced myself that "this time will be the last time" with whatever temptation I was facing on a particular day. The problem should be obvious—every time I give in, I am weaker the next time. So, it gets easier and easier to say, "maybe just once more." I think part of why I got into this pattern is that the thought of letting go of something for good just felt too overwhelming.

BE FREE

The good news is it also works in reverse. Jesus said, "Don't worry about tomorrow, for tomorrow will bring worries of its own" (Matthew 6:34). All we can do is face today. So, if my only job is to face the thing coming at me today, it doesn't seem so overwhelming. I don't have to think about resisting a thousand times. I am just resisting one time. And a positive bi-product of that is it will get easier each time because I am getting stronger in God every moment I choose him.

Pay Attention to Hunger Pains
It is a mistake to think that all desire is evil. We can have deep desires that are very good. The psalmist wrote, "Take delight in the LORD, and he will give you the desires of your heart" (Psalm 37:4). This means that desire is not the problem; it is when our desires get misdirected that we get into trouble.

I have learned that if I am feeling a strong desire or temptation to sin, it is likely that there is a good desire underneath the surface. The truth is, I am hungry for God and the life he offers. The way I am responding to that hunger is to look at what is within arm's reach, but my real desire is for God.

When I begin to feel a strong pull toward something, I try to pay attention and allow that hunger pain to serve as a flare that goes off in my mind. It is a warning signal that my soul is dry. In this way, I can actually take the temptation and use it to my advantage.

The next thing to do is to take that need to God. And we are almost ready to begin looking at how to enter fully into this life-giving relationship with God. But first, there is one more tactic of the enemy we need to address. We've seen the enemy is trying to isolate us from God to keep us in bondage. If he can't get us alone by leading us away from God, he will often try to make us think we are alone by suggesting God has abandoned us. To accomplish this, he will use fear and intimidation.

CHAPTER 8

TALLER THAN A TOWER
CONQUERING FEAR

I can visit any news website and within five minutes, I will know about new causes of cancer, several reasons why whichever president is in office is destroying the nation, and how long I have to pack my car before a pending nuclear war breaks out. The dominant world view (at least in American culture) is exceedingly fear-based and hopeless. And the negativity is not just related to the current state of things, but it extends to the future. People all around us are striving for enough material security to ensure protection from future calamity.

Satan also plays a role in this. Jesus called him the ruler of this world (John 14:30) and Paul called him the ruler of the power of the air (Ephesians 2:2). So, if the atmosphere of our world is one of fear, stress, worry, and anxiety, it stands to reason that Satan has a hand in setting this tone. Just like the media, he puts his spin on everything. The best way to describe this tactic is intimidation. Intimidation leads to fear and fear will separate us from God and take us back into sin.

First, I want to clarify that it is normal to experience fear—like when my wife grabs my shoulder because I swerved near the center line. There are completely valid experiences that prompt fear, worry, and stress. Trials are taking place in our lives and world that evoke these emotions. But the question is: what do we do with them? When in the fire, we have a tendency to believe God has abandoned us. This will erode our trust in him and leave us feeling alone. And the belief that we are alone will inevitably take us deeper into fear. It can become our default position.

Then every difficulty that comes (even small ones) will simply reinforce our belief that we are alone and add on to the fear. It is like quicksand, and it steals the life God has for us. Jesus once told a parable of a man sowing seeds. Some fell on the path, and the birds swallowed them. Others fell onto rocky soil, and they grew quickly, but the sun scorched them because they had no roots. Then there were seeds that fell among thorns. As the plants grew, the thorns choked them out. Jesus explained that the seeds are God's words, and the thorns represented the "cares of the world" (Matthew 13).

The "cares of this world" (or fears) begin to cut us off from the life of God. And as we have seen time and time again, in the absence (or at least perceived absence) of God, we are far more likely to return to sin.

FEAR LEADS US BACK INTO SIN

One day I was alone and I felt the Holy Spirit prompt a thought in my mind that surprised me. The thought was that most of my struggle with sin could be tied back to fear. That seemed like a large claim, but then I began to think it through, and it made sense.

If I am living under worry and fear, I am more easily prone to seek escape or at least something to calm my nerves. I talked before about the idea of self-medicating with attachments. My former attachments can look like a drug or a balm. They begin to seem very appealing when I am under stress, even though I know they will only bring temporary relief. In addition to making me more susceptible to my old habits, fear impacts my relationships.

When we become consumed by fear, it takes us into independence. And when we live independently from God out of a feeling of abandonment, we tend to shift into preservation mode. We act like a wounded animal that is self-protective and solely interested in survival. As a result I am edgier and more likely to lash out at the people I am in relationship with who are not doing what I want (or who are doing things I don't want).

For much of our marriage, my wife and I have felt the stress of money. I need to qualify this by acknowledging that even in our lowest moments, we still had more material security than the majority of the world. But it has been a struggle nonetheless. Buying groceries often felt traumatic. I remember walking to the store on my lunch breaks and staring at the lottery tickets. I would see myself scratching away the silver dust to reveal a sum of money that I thought would bring us peace.

I lived in constant fear that we wouldn't have enough, and it would be my fault. I knew I wasn't supposed to worry about what we would eat or what we would wear (Matthew 6:25) but I still did. Because of this constant stress, I did not navigate conflict well. I was often harsh and unkind to my wife in arguments. This behavior could almost always be tied back to my fear. I believed I was alone, it was up to me to do better next time, which obviously never worked.

This is why Paul said, ". . . whatever does not proceed from faith is sin" (Romans 14:23). In other words, when our trust in God is eroded because of fear, we will act and live apart from God, which takes us into sin. So, what is the solution? How do we overcome fear?

FEAR NOT

Often times when an angel shows up in the Bible, the first thing the angel says is not to be afraid (Luke 2:10). Jesus said the same thing when he first called his disciples to follow him (Luke 5:10) and also when he appeared to them after he'd risen from death. Luke wrote,

> Jesus himself stood among them and said to them, "Peace be with you." They were startled and terrified, and thought that they were seeing a ghost. He said to them, "Why are you frightened, and why do doubts arise in your hearts? Look at my hands and my feet; see that it is I myself." —Luke 24:36–39

It would seem like the most common Biblical advice for dealing with fear is to simply stop being afraid. This seems like strange advice at first. We all know you can't just tell someone to turn off their fear. It doesn't work.

For example, after dinner we usually instruct our kids to go upstairs to get ready for bed. They don't always finish eating at the same time, so occasionally, one of my kids will receive this instruction before the others. A few minutes will pass, and I will look out of the kitchen and find that instead of brushing his or her teeth, this child is sitting on the bottom step, looking into the kitchen. And the reason, as you've probably guessed, is that they feel afraid. Though I should know better, I've tried many times to convince them that the upstairs is no different whether it is day or night. It is an impossible conversation and, in the end, there is only one thing that will cause the child to move from the step—if someone goes with them.

"I'M NOT AFRAID OF ANYTHING"

One day, our four-year-old son, JJ, was standing next to the car when he noticed some type of communication tower not far in the distance. He cranked his head back to look up at the tower and then turned to look back at Heather. "Mom," he said, "that tower is taller than Dad, right?" Now, if JJ had left off the last word, I never would have thought anything of it. But the fact that he ended with "right?" meant he wasn't stating it as much as he was asking it. He was trying to verify his assessment of my height in relation to the tower. While he was correct, the tower was taller than me, it was close enough that he had to run it past Mom. This meant from JJ's perspective, I am pretty tall.

A few days after the tower discussion, we were all riding in the car without much conversation. Then, without any apparent prompting, JJ said, "Dad, I'm not afraid of anything." While JJ does fear some things, his statement was fairly accurate. He is the kid who will jump from the top step with nothing but a rolled-up sweatshirt to soften the landing. I affirmed his courage, and we went on with the day.

It wasn't until later that I realized these two stories were connected. I sensed the Holy Spirit showing me that the fact that JJ is rather fearless is directly related to the fact that he believes his dad to be almost as tall as a 200-foot tower. If we know someone is with us who is big enough to protect us from harm, we tend to feel less afraid. In other words, when we know we are not alone, fear generally goes away.

When Jesus asked his friends why they were afraid, I don't believe he was saying "What is wrong with you? Just snap out of it." It was more like, "Hey guys, it's me. I'm back. You've got nothing to worry about because I am with you." They thought he was dead and believed they were seeing a ghost. Said another way, they thought they were alone. But Jesus invited them to feel his hands and side. He confirmed he was actually with them.

Though the time did come for Jesus to return to heaven, he made a promise before leaving. He instructed them make disciples of nations, and then said to them, ". . . remember, I am with you always, to the end of the age" (Matthew 28:20). Though he was returning to heaven, Jesus was not leaving them alone. Before his death he'd told the disciples that he would be sending them the Holy Spirit (John 16:7–15). And this Spirit did come to Jesus' friends shortly after he left (Acts 2). This is the reason Jesus could tell his friends not to be afraid—because they were not alone. If we can understand and know he is with us, fear leaves. As the Old Testament author wrote, "Be strong and courageous; do not be frightened or dismayed, for the LORD your God is with you wherever you go" (Joshua 1:9).

I want to pause and clarify that I am not saying that because we have the Holy Spirit, followers of Jesus are immune from suffering. Jesus said that we would face trials (John 16:33) and he also said that

BE FREE

tomorrow will bring worries of its own (Matthew 6:34). But I would like us to consider for a moment what would be the greatest trial any of us could face. I would argue that death is the thing we fear more than any other. And we already know that Jesus has abolished death (2 Timothy 1:10). Death no longer has the last word. So if our God has defeated the most formidable enemy we could face and this same death-defying Spirit lives in us (Romans 8:11), what do we actually have to fear?

The one who is with us is taller than a 200-foot tower, and if he can help us overcome death, he can help us overcome anything. He can bring resurrection to every part of our lives. Because he is with us in every trial, good can come from anything we face. God has the ability to take things that were intended for evil and turn them for good (Genesis 50:20). We still live in a world broken by sin and under the deception of the enemy. But we are talking about a God who brings good out of evil. I like to say that God can make gold from mud. If we have trouble seeing how God is doing this in our lives, it may be because we are misunderstanding or misinterpreting the way God works in our trials.

LEAPING OVER WALLS

One of the things that causes us to doubt God's presence is when we face a trial that won't go away. There have been times I've felt like I was running into a wall that I couldn't move.

TALLER THAN A TOWER

I wanted God to just knock it over so I could forge ahead. But eventually, I realized God wanted me to turn to him so we could go over the wall together. The psalmist wrote, ". . . by my God I can leap over a wall" (Psalm 18:29). A wall is not evidence that God has abandoned us—he will never leave us. This world has walls in it. The question is whether we will turn to the One who is bigger than the walls.

The next thing God has the ability to do through a trial is strengthen us. I want to be clear—I do not believe that God causes terrible things to happen to people to make them stronger. Many of the trials we walk through are the result of human sin or the work of Satan. What I am saying is that God has the power and wisdom to capitalize on the trials we endure in order to strengthen us in him.

In the physical realm, we build strength when the fibers in our muscles are torn due to stress and resistance. When the fibers fuse back together, additional muscle tissue is created and we become stronger. I believe God can build our spirits in the same way. The point is, the resistance we feel in this process toward freedom actually makes us stronger. We can have hope that every time we turn to God, we are getting stronger, and it will be easier next time. This strengthening process is helping us become the person he created us to be. He is literally rebuilding us. Paul said he boasted in his suffering because: "Suffering produces endurance, and endurance produces character, and character produces hope, and hope does not disappoint us, because God's love has been poured into our hearts through the Holy Spirit that has been given to us." (Romans 5:3–5)

There is a scene in one of Lewis' Narnia books where Susan climbs a tree to escape a wolf sent by the White Witch. When Peter first realizes what is going on, Aslan's soldiers begin to advance on the wolf, but Aslan calls them off, saying, "Back! Let the Prince win his spurs." With the reassurance of the great lion, Peter begins to run toward the wolf, who is part way up the tree and thrashing at Susan with an open mouth. Aslan is not far off but allows Peter to face the wolf. In a blur of fear and confusion, Peter manages to put his sword through the animal and save not only himself, but also his sister.[1]

BE FREE

Aslan could have killed the wolf easily, knocking him down and crushing him under the weight of his paw. But he didn't because he wanted Peter to fight. He knew Peter could win because he had everything he needed. Aslan was there with him, and he was the one who gave the sword to Peter in the first place. He was Peter's rear guard for the entire battle (Isaiah 52:12). This, I believe, is how God often works with us. If you have trouble relating to the analogy of killing a wolf, maybe it would be easier to talk about learning to drive.

I once tried to drive on my own when I was eleven or twelve years old. My family was getting ready for church and running a bit late. So I climbed into the minivan, which was parked in the garage. I was thinking I would help by backing out the vehicle. Instead of putting the van into reverse, I put it in drive and rolled forward into the shelves that lined the back wall of the garage. I was only able to go forward a few feet before the van stopped. Normally this would not have been a major problem. But the force of the van actually tipped the shelf forward, causing it to hit the aluminum canoe that was hanging from the ceiling in the back of the garage. This caused one of the chains to break and the canoe came down like a trap door on a hinge. It landed squarely on the front hood, leaving a substantial dent. I learned a valuable lesson; I needed to be with someone who knew more about driving than me.

My first lessons came from my dad. I remember driving around an empty parking lot and killing a couple of orange cones while trying to parallel park. Several years after getting my license, I met Heather. The summer we met, she taught me how to drive a stick. And the truth is, she's been teaching me about driving ever since. I drive much better when she is with me. Just the other night, we were coming home in the dark and she spotted the shinning eyes of a deer standing in the ditch. She grew up in the woods of Wisconsin, and her dad taught her to see in the dark. Not only do I need her help, but the journey is way more fulfilling with her in the car than it could ever be driving alone.

The key is for us to walk with God. It is about unity and relationship. This is how we win the battles against the devil and the world and the flesh. This is how we experience the freedom promised to us. If we can believe he is with us and experience his presence, fear will no longer control us. But how do we get there? You can't just force yourself to believe something. Trust will come out of a real relationship with God. So now we'll look at how that can happen on a practical level.

I've been using metaphors, which are helpful in illustrating a concept, but are limited in two ways. First, the metaphors I share don't give the full picture. It is true that we can walk with God in relationship, but there is more. He doesn't just offer to walk with us like a spouse or a friend. He offers to live in us (Romans 8:10). He can put his life and his spirit in our bodies, and our minds can be united with his mind (1 Corinthians 2:16). This is a concept that moves beyond a familiar metaphor. The second issue with using metaphors is that they are not very practical. We need to see what all of this means in the real world. What are the tangible, specific things we can do each day to walk with God and allow God to live in us? How does this work each morning when we wake up and step into the day? These are important questions, because we can't see him.

It is easy to fall into the lie that it is impossible to relate to God or experience his power and life in a real, concrete way. This is, of course, untrue. It is possible to rebuild a covenant relationship with God that can be experienced in tangible ways. It is possible to be united with him so that our lives become infused with his life. And once this starts to happen, true freedom begins. Now it is time to find out how.

CHAPTER 9

THE MAN WHO BOUGHT A FIELD
OPENING UP TO GOD

EMPTYING OURSELVES

How do we begin to form a relationship with God so his life can flow in us and through us? The first thing is to begin to make room. We are full, but need to empty ourselves so we are positioned to receive him. The more we have of God and his life, the freer we will become. Part of why we don't experience God's power and presence tangibly is because we are filled with so many other things. We are saturated. Our stomachs are filled with food. Our heads are filled with images and noise. And our days are filled with work and media and a million other distractions. These are all the things we've gone to for fulfillment apart from God. Even if some of them are good, they are out of order. I once heard a man say, "We've got our priorities crooked."

To receive life from God, we need to learn how to detach more and more from the other things we've gone to for life. We need to literally empty ourselves. Gerald May wrote that we need to have a posture of relinquishment, which will create a spaciousness for God's grace to enter in.[1] Then his power can run into us and through us like water flowing through an unblocked pipe. When we have space for his presence to enter, we can begin to build unity with him.

We've talked about the importance of letting go and returning to dependence on God. But now let's look at the specific process that allows this to happen.

To break the power of an addiction or attachment, we do have to actually stop the behavior.[2] We need to think of it as releasing the old so we can take hold of the new. We must make space for God to enter so he can fill us. But how do we stop? Or maybe the better question is, where do we start?

BE FREE

TREASURE IN A FIELD

The first thing we need is a vision. We need to obtain a picture of what we are aiming for. Our focus should not be on what we are trying to walk away from but rather on what we are walking toward. This is a trade. We are choosing to die, so we can live.

Jesus told a story about a man who sold everything he had to buy a field. To an outside observer, this may seem crazy. Who would trade all they have for a bunch of dirt? But the man knew something about this field. He knew that buried in the field was a treasure that was more valuable than anything he'd ever seen (Matthew 13:44). If we understand the value of the treasure, it would be foolish not to give up everything to buy the field.

Remember the rich young ruler we talked about before? When Jesus asked him to sell everything, he walked away. The reason, I think, is because he didn't see the true worth of the treasure. He didn't fully understand what he had to gain in exchange for giving up his attachments. But there was another rich man who responded differently when he met Jesus.

Zacchaeus was a chief tax collector and was wealthy because of his profession. Jesus decided he wanted to stay at the house of Zacchaeus and the tax collector welcomed him. After meeting Jesus, the man declared that he would give away half of his possessions and vowed that if he had cheated anyone, he would pay them back four times the amount (Luke 19:1–8). As far as we can tell, Jesus didn't even ask him to do this. I think what changed Zacchaeus was that he saw the treasure.

Imagine a life where you could stand up straight because you no longer struggle with the same old sins (Romans 6:11). A life that is completely free of shame and condemnation (Romans 8:1). Imagine experiencing complete peace in the face of every trial and circumstance (Philippians 4:7) and a joy that gives you strength (Nehemiah 8:10). This life is available in Jesus. It is called the kingdom of God. God created many things that are good gifts given for our enjoyment. When we are getting our fulfillment from God, we can enjoy the good things he made in the right way. These things can be reminders of his goodness that point us back to him. Jesus said to strive first for the kingdom and everything else will also be given (Matthew 6:33). Paul described the treasure found in Jesus as "boundless riches" (Ephesians 3:8). Once we have a clear vision of the treasure, we must make the choice to act.

ENGAGING THE WILL

Paul said, "No longer present your members to sin as instruments of wickedness . . ." (Romans 6:13). The fact that Paul offers this as instruction tells us we can follow it. We said in chapter 7 that we have to take an active role in breaking our sin habits. We must engage our will again and become decisive. May wrote that we must have a "willingness to enter the deserts of our lives [and] to commit ourselves to struggle with attachment."[3]

As we've seen, we can't make it on willpower alone. I am not talking about a fierce self-determination. This is a process we enter into with the Holy Spirit, which presents us with a challenging paradox. To be filled with God, we need to make room for his Spirit. But to release our attachments and thereby open up the space, we need the power of his Spirit. In other words, we need more of God to receive more of God. So then how does the plane ever get off the ground? It is actually pretty simple.

The focus should not be on trying to stop a certain sin. Instead, it should be on releasing the sin so we can make room for God. The function of our will is to connect us to God. If we are moving toward God, we will automatically be moving away from the lessor things. Remember, the definition of sin is to miss the mark. So the opposite of this would be to aim for God. In practice, I am still letting go of certain behaviors, but the focus is on what I'm gaining, not on what I'm losing.

While the concept sounds very basic, putting it into practice can still be a bit challenging because, at times, we feel bombarded by our desires and by the endless opportunities to sin. When all our old attachments are calling to us and the offerings of this world are swarming around our heads, it can feel like we live in a fog. All the things we thought we wanted fill the air like smoke, and it is hard to get our bearings. In this place, we feel like we want to sin more than we want God. The answer is to look for moments of clarity.

One day I was driving in a hard rain. I couldn't discern the individual drops of water. The rain was so thick it was like driving in a lake. I felt submerged. The wiper blades whipped back and forth frantically and accomplished nothing. But then I went under an overpass. Beneath the shelter of the intersecting road, I could see clearly for a few seconds. The pounding stopped and the world came back. My drowning vehicle was able to come up for air just long enough to confirm I was still on the road.

We all have moments of clarity when we don't feel a strong pull toward old things, and we realize our true desire is for Jesus. At times we will feel like David when he wrote, "I delight to do your will, O my God" (Psalm 40:8). Even for someone who has not made the initial decision to surrender to Jesus and doesn't feel a discernible desire to find God, there are moments where there is a desire for freedom, or at least for something better. There is the recognition that something isn't right. Paul talked about the ways of God being written on our hearts, even if we don't know him yet (Romans 2:14–15).

Depending on your story and the attachments you face, these moments of clarity may be rare, but they are still there. A spark always remains. There is always the hope of finding our way back out of prison. Paul wrote, "but with the testing he will also provide the way out so that you may be able to endure it" (1 Corinthians 10:13). If this wasn't true, none of us would ever get free.

These are the moments we need to capitalize on. When the rain lifts and we can see the choices up ahead. In these moments, when our will is already turned toward God, we choose to release the old. It is much easier to make the decision when we are not in the middle of a disorienting storm. Here are some practical ways to do this.

THE MAN WHO BOUGHT A FIELD

THINGS TO DO IN A MOMENT OF CLARITY

Seek Intervention.
At times, we need to seek help. The truth is, we need each other. We will cover this more fully in Chapter 11. But I mention it now because there are certain addictions and attachments that require intervention. If a person is addicted to powerful substances that have a dangerous potential for backlash, it is important to seek "medically supervised tapering."[4] There are organizations that have solid structures in place to offer this kind of help.

Plan a Different Route.
Next, consider the value of having a plan. The idea is to make decisions in advance to stay away from the situations we know will bring temptation. Say no to the precursors to temptation. I compare this to the rudder on a ship. Small corrections made in advance are far more effective than drastic measures taken at the point of crisis. When we are clear-headed, we can make decisions to let go before we are actually in the situation. I heard a pastor telling a story about his friend who was working on getting free from alcohol. For any who have been there, you know it is a fierce attachment to break. He kept relapsing and wasn't sure what to do. Then he realized that on his drive to work every day, he passed two different liquor stores. This meant he was driving through the war zone four times a day. He made a simple decision during a moment of clarity to find a different route to work.

Pull Up the Roots.
There is a movie I saw once about a married couple on the brink of divorce. One of the issues was the husband's addiction to pornography. There is a powerful scene where he takes preventative action in a moment of clarity. The man is pacing around his living room and his computer is sitting on a table across the room. You can see his struggle, it is like there are invisible arms reaching out of the monitor and pulling at his head. But then something shifts within him, and a resolve settles on his face. The husband turns toward his desk and

picks up the computer. He rips it from the wall, storms outside, and throws the computer onto the ground. Then he grabs a baseball bat and swings wildly at the machine like he is killing a bear. Pieces of plastic and metal are floating past him, and he keeps swinging until he is sure it is dead.

While eliminating the conduit of the temptation is helpful, we still have the challenge tied to the specific attachment we are trying to break. Even if our focus is on letting go of the old in order to take hold of God, we still have to engage directly with the specific sin. The good news is the decision to make space for God does not always need to be tied to a specific attachment. This leads us to a concept called redirection.

REDIRECTION

There is an important set of practices found throughout the history of the church called spiritual disciplines. The phrase can sound off-putting, but these practices have the potential to open us up for major breakthroughs and freedom. They are things that Jesus, Paul, and countless others have modeled for us. Paul said that he punished or disciplined his body to receive an "imperishable wreath" (1 Corinthians 9:25–27). Paul was not talking about self-abuse. He was talking about withholding certain things from the self in order to be filled by eternal things. It doesn't feel like discipline when our eye is on the prize. Willard refers to these practices as the disciplines of abstinence.[5] When we make space for God, we will become more filled with God, and we have less of an appetite from the lesser things. Even if the thing we remove doesn't tie directly to an attachment, it can still help free us from that attachment. There are many different practices, but I want to focus on the three that are the most practical and helpful to me. They are silence, solitude, and fasting.

Silence and Solitude

We live like salmon. The river is loud and there are a lot of fish rubbing up against us. Noise is not bad, but it is distracting. It is hard to think clearly when sound waves are constantly vibrating inside our heads. It is also not bad to be around people. Relationships with people are vital to our freedom (as we will see in chapter 11). But it is important to find moments when we move away from people temporarily. Jesus sometimes went up the side of a mountain to be alone and quiet with God (Luke 6:12). This decision to detach makes it easier to look to God for life because there is less competition. In fact, it is vital we have regular moments like this so we can be filled by the Spirit.

I should mention that silence and solitude are not the same thing. It is possible to be alone in your house, for example, and still turn on the TV. It is also possible to be around other people and remain in silence—like during the middle of the night. It is great to seek both at once, but that may not always be possible.

It is rare in our culture to go into a place where we are completely alone and quiet. Practically, it is hard to do. We have to be creative. At the advice of a friend, I stopped listening to the radio in the car. Twice a day, I am alone in the car in the quiet. The silence is unnerving at first. But it does eventually turn into peace.

Silence in the car doesn't work for everyone. Heather usually has five other humans with her anytime she is driving. Once she was in the car with our kids and somehow, over all the other noise, she heard the sound of liquid trickling down the vinyl seats. One of the kids hadn't made it home to use the bathroom. Needless to say, Heather finds her quiet at night when the kids have gone to sleep.

I've also started climbing trees to find silence and solitude. Generally, there aren't too many people thirty feet in the air. The only sound is the wind pushing the leaves, causing them to hit each other like a million clapping hands. I think this is why people build temples on the tops of mountains.

While silence and solitude are helpful, possibly one of the most powerful practices available to us is fasting.

BE FREE

Fasting

The practice of fasting involves going a period of time without food, or at least without certain foods. In the Old Testament, Daniel engaged in a fast where he ate only vegetables (Daniel 1:12). Some of the desert fathers, such as St. Antony, would go for long periods of time on just bread and water. But often a fast involves a voluntary decision to go without any food at all. The time frame also varies. Generally, when I've fasted, it has been for one or two days, although people have survived up to forty days without food.[6]

The goal in fasting is not to make us more favored by God. It is not an exercise in superiority. God often told Israel the fasting he preferred was to do justice and to let the oppressed go free (Isaiah 58:6). Jesus also made it clear that the purpose is not to get approval from people (Matthew 6:16).

Instead, the goal is to help separate from one of our most basic physical needs to bring us into a place of dependence on God. Our need for food is so prevalent, we don't realize how often we think about it until we aren't eating. To help illustrate, I'd like to share some of the things I encountered last time I fasted.

On the first morning of the fast, I woke up with an excitement that was followed immediately by disappointment. I realized the excitement was for breakfast, and it left when I realized I wouldn't be eating. Then when I got to work, I saw pastries on the office kitchen table. In the space where I work, there is a mini fridge. I am used to walking over there several times a day. Instead I just stared at it. An hour or so later I read an email about free pizza, which was followed by an email about the new coffee machine. At this point, the day started to blur together, but I remember someone carrying a plate of steaming chicken past me. I finally went outside to escape the food assault. The first thing I smelled was a hamburger over a flame. Across the parking lot I saw the Perkins restaurant that had always been there, but I'd never really looked at. There is a giant American flag outside the restaurant that was waving at me as if beckoning me to come over. I started thinking about the last time I ate there in college, and how a taco salad sounded really good. The point is, my day was consumed with thoughts about food. I realized that this was the same as most days except now I was aware of it.

The process helped me realize what things dominate my mind and fill my life, and how this keeps me from opening myself to God's Spirit. As the basic need of food, for example, is removed, it does something to open the mind and heart to God and he becomes our food (John 4:32). When we begin to taste the life God offers, it gives us power to let go of lesser things.

We looked previously at how the Spirit led Jesus out into the wilderness after his baptism. But we didn't consider that he had fasted for forty days before the devil came and began to tempt him. I've heard many people say that Jesus must have been at his weakest during this battle. He must have been so hungry that the stones around him already looked like bread, even before the tempter suggested the idea. But recently I heard a different interpretation. Though the devil probably thought Jesus was weak when he came to confront him, Jesus was not at his weakest, he was at his strongest. He said to the devil, "One does not live by bread alone but by every word that comes from the mouth of God" (Matthew 4:4). A different time, Jesus told his disciples he had a food they did not know about (John 4:32). The result of going without food for forty days was that Jesus became filled with the Holy Spirit. During his fast, Jesus strengthened his connection to the Father. He was feeding on God. I mentioned that the Spirit led Jesus into the wilderness, but the writers also told us that he left the wilderness filled with the power of the Spirit (Luke 4:14).

So it is with us. If we empty ourselves, we can be filled with God's Spirit. Jesus said he is the bread of life (John 6:35). He is our food. When we become empty of other things, we can finally begin to experience his presence and his power. Paul said that the kingdom of God is not food and drink but righteousness and peace and joy in the Holy Spirit (Romans 14:17).

This does not mean it won't be a struggle. God still requires a sacrifice to buy the field. But it is well worth it because we know about the treasure buried there.

BE FREE

IT IS WELL WORTH IT

As we engage in the process of making space for God's Spirit, whether detaching from specific things or engaging in more general disciplines, we will likely experience withdrawal before the beautiful breakthrough comes. This withdrawal can be physical, mental, and/or emotional.

At times I've experienced intense physical symptoms when detaching from things. During one season, I was abstaining from all sugar. On the first day, I developed a progressive headache. It started as a subtle pulse that swelled by lunch. I had trouble walking and had to keep my eyes closed. Lying down magnified the throbbing. It eventually graduated into a migraine, and I lost most of the healthy food I'd eaten that day. Headaches are also common for me when I've fasted from food, though not always so intense. Fasting also affects the stomach. Obviously, you feel hunger and fatigue. But possibly the strangest physical symptom I've experienced during a fast was a burning in my stomach and esophagus—almost like heartburn. I felt like little men with torches were crawling through my chest.

I've also often experienced strange thoughts and feelings during the detachment process. One time I decided to fast on a Sunday. We were at church and the kids asked about getting donuts. As I walked behind them, I noticed they were dropping large chunks of donut on the ground. I had only been fasting a few hours and I pictured myself diving at the ground and licking the floor.

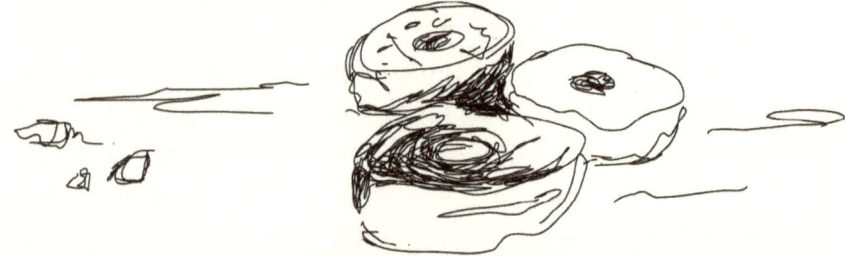

Previously I mentioned feeling disappointment over not being able to eat during a fast; that is just one of many emotions that tends to surface. I've also experienced fear and panic over the thought of not eating. I've even felt apathy and disdain. During one fast, I was at my kids' school and was sitting on an old couch that was sucking me into the cushions. An older woman asked me to move because they were trying to set up for a blood drive. Normally I would have made a point to respond with kindness, but I am not sure I even responded at all. I may have made a noise, but it wasn't words. I packed up and left with my head down and fists in my pockets. Most of the day I felt apathetic and annoyed with the world. I was even bothered by the shoes people were wearing.

Depending on your story, the symptoms of withdrawal may be more intense than what I've described. But the good news is, it gets easier. If we can make the choice to stay with this process, the pain will pass. The grip of our old attachments will begin to loosen. As the demands of flesh are denied, they weaken—it is death by starvation. Not only does the pain subside, but we begin to wake up to what we've been missing.

I once watched a science-fiction movie where the government required all citizens to take a daily sedative. Everyone became numb and cold and the world looked gray. But then the hero of the story decides to throw away the drug. First his eyes become sensitive to light. Then he begins to see color, and he notices the feeling of a metal railing under his hand. In the same way, our attachments have often numbed us to the life God is offering.

As we wake up, we start to look at things differently. We can enjoy the things God is giving us because we are no longer trying to get our life from them. Our life comes from him.

As difficult as it has been for me to fast, I always reach a point where the hunger ceases, and I begin to turn my thoughts to God. Though I generally face the fridge for the first half, I find myself facing God by the end. And then when the fast is over, I approach food differently—at least for a while. I have a gratitude for it without feeling an obsession over it. Once, I noticed myself marveling at the flavor of a carrot. Food actually tastes better when I am not using it to get full, because I am already full from God.

The same thing happens with solitude and silence. Sometimes

extended silence is almost unbearable for me. The lull of nothing can feel more intense than sitting in a stadium filled with people. Once I was alone at a cabin with no Internet or TV or music.

Then I went outside and realized there was a choir flying over my head. The sunlight found a tunnel through a wall of trees two hundred feet thick. And I had a sense God was filling me with the noise and the presence of heaven. He was filling me with himself.

In describing the taste of a carrot or the sound of a bird, I am aware of how small those things seem. But all of reality can begin to change as we make room for more of God's life to enter. We start looking at things differently. And as we begin to experience the boundless riches of love, joy, peace, and hope, the old things we used to fill ourselves with lose their appeal. This is why Paul regarded everything as loss in comparison to the "surpassing value of knowing Jesus" (Philippians 3:8).

The key here is we really can't begin to experience the things I am describing until we have stepped away from the lesser things. We have to risk first and then the reward follows. When we start to empty ourselves, it seems at first like we are getting weaker. But we are actually putting ourselves in a position to get stronger and fuller.

Even as we get stronger, we need to remember this is still a process. At times, the old things may still feel desirable and seem more accessible. But even this we can use to our advantage. Those who specialize in the science of changing habits say you need a trigger to change a behavior.[7] The old longings that rise up can serve as this trigger. When our "hunger" pains rise up, we can learn to treat them as signals going off in our minds to remind us we are actually hungry for God. And then we can go to him to be filled.

So how do we do that practically? How do we eat the words that come from the mouth of God? How do we commune with him and have a relationship with him? We've looked at how to empty ourselves to make room for God, now let's look at proactive things we can do to become more filled with his Spirit.

CHAPTER 10

SITTING ON A SONG
BEING FILLED BY THE SPIRIT

LEARNING TO LIVE BY THE SPIRIT

When we detach and flee from lesser things, it opens up space within us for God's Spirit to flood in like air filling a vacuum. And as the Spirit fills us, we begin to experience true freedom.

Jesus said he would send us an advocate (John 14:16) and this Spirit would guide us into all truth (John 16:13). John said knowing the truth sets us free (John 8:32). We saw that knowing the truth involves right thinking about who God is and who we are. As the Holy Spirit guides us, our thinking begins to change, and our view of reality gets corrected. When we become more confident in who Jesus is and what he thinks about us, it will begin to change how we live because our thoughts and emotions direct our actions. This allows us to recognize and refute the lies that keep us in prison.

But also remember that knowing the truth is not just about changing our minds. To know the truth is to know a person. Jesus said that he is the truth (John 14:6). He said that we can be connected to him like a branch to a vine (John 15:5). We can receive life from him because his life can flow through us. The same Spirit that lives in Jesus actual dwells in us (2 Corinthians 13:5). This is where the power to walk in freedom really comes from.

The Holy Spirit makes freedom a reality because it guides us into relationship with Jesus and then helps keep us there. Our job, then, is to learn to live according to the Spirit as Paul said (Romans 8:4). As we discuss how the Spirit interacts with us, we will move along on a spectrum from concrete to more abstract and experiential. Both are important. The first way the Holy Spirit has revealed Jesus to us is through the Bible.

BE FREE

BIBLE: KNOWING VS. KNOWLEDGE

The most tangible tool available to help us build a relationship with Jesus is the Bible.

It is the record of God's interaction with us. The Bible provides us with important knowledge of who God is and what he thinks of us. In the Bible, God also shows us the example of how he wants us to live. In other words, it reveals the life that is available to us. It is not a book of theories, it is a practical guide about real life. One of the reasons I am convinced the Bible is true is because it works. Every time I've decided to remove the log in my own eye instead of the speck in my brother's eye, it has helped heal my relationships (Luke 6:42).

While I believe it is a practical book, not everything in the Bible is self-explanatory. For this reason, it is important to gain an understanding of what we are reading. It is even helpful to study the original languages, the cultural contexts, and so forth. Many people have a variety of things to say about this book, and some are not helpful. Thus, the goal is to know as much as we can. Having said all of that, here are a couple of important points.

First, you don't have to be a linguist, a sociologist, or a theologian to benefit from reading the Bible. I believe that the gospel stories reveal who God is in Jesus in a rather straightforward way. Additionally, it is possible to benefit from reading the Bible even if we don't fully grasp everything it is saying (none of us do, by the way). Pastor Bill Johnson often points out that you can benefit from eating a banana even if you don't understand the biology behind the digestion process. Jesus said we live on every word that comes from the mouth of God (Matthew 4:4, Deuteronomy 8:3).

Second, and most importantly, we need to realize that gaining knowledge about God and/or how he wants us to live is not an end in itself. We should not read the Bible solely to gain knowledge. If we do, we've missed the whole point. Jesus said to religious scholars, "You search the scriptures because you think that in them you have eternal life; and it is they that testify on my behalf. Yet you refuse to come to me to have life" (John 5:39–40).

SITTING ON A SONG

The Bible is not meant to save us; it is meant to point to the one who does. It testifies to Jesus and Jesus reveals the invisible God (Colossians 1:15). The knowledge we gain about God through Jesus is meant to lead us into relationship with him. The goal is not to know *about* Jesus but to know him personally.

To treat God like a topic to be studied is to miss the life he offers. My kids found a dead dragonfly one day and brought it into the house. They kept it in a dish for weeks. We learned some things about that insect as it sat lifeless in the glass dish, but I can't say we got to know him (or her). The last thing we want to do is treat God like this dragonfly.

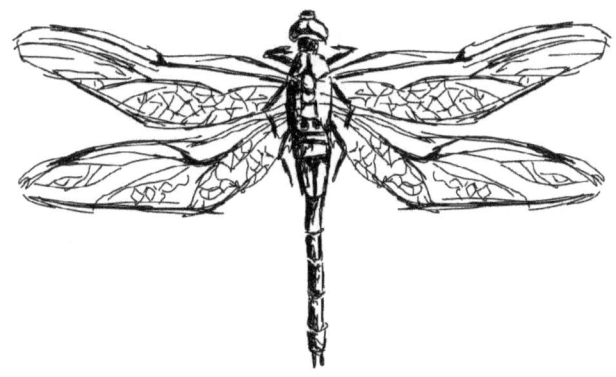

We can't pin Jesus to a board or place him in a dish. He is alive and he wants to be known. And as we get to know him, it changes us. There is a story in Acts that illustrates what happens to people who truly know Jesus. Peter and John had been arrested for teaching the people the Gospel. We are told that as Peter was talking to his accusers, they "saw the boldness of Peter and John and realized that they were uneducated and ordinary men [but] they were amazed and recognized them as companions of Jesus" (Acts 4:13). Peter and John didn't have a formal education and probably had less head knowledge than the religious leaders accusing them (the same leaders who searched the scriptures for eternal life). And yet they amazed these religious leaders because of their boldness and power to heal. Peter and John were different because they knew Jesus and because they were filled with

BE FREE

the Holy Spirit (Acts 4:8). The people recognized they'd been with Jesus because they were doing the same things Jesus did. His life was literally flowing through them.

We tend to become like the people we look up to and spend time with because they exercise the greatest influence on us. So, the first thing to do is to read the stories of Jesus over and over. This is what it means to meditate on God's word (Psalm 1:2). The more familiar we are with Jesus' character, the more it will impact our character. In other words, the more we get to know him, the more we will begin to think and act like him.

LEARNING FROM EXAMPLE

I've already mentioned that I struggle with defensiveness. I am very familiar with James' instruction about being quick to listen and slow to speak (James 1:19). However, this is easier said than done. What really started to help me was meditating on the story of Jesus' trial. After he was arrested, the leaders brought Jesus before Pilate for questioning. The mob and the religious leaders shouted accusations against him. He had done nothing wrong and was without sin (2 Corinthians 5:21). But even though he was innocent, Jesus hardly said anything in defense (Luke 23:9). I become defensive even when I have done wrong and just don't want to admit it. I've literally given long speeches in my own defense. And Jesus, an innocent man being sentenced to death, didn't respond. He was filled with courage and humility and self-control. James said be slow to speak but Jesus showed us what this looks like.

To give another example, Jesus showed what it looks like to dignify people. He had many interactions with women. At least some of these women were accustomed to being used by men. The Samaritan woman, for example, had been rejected by at least five husbands (John 4). Most men would have either ignored her or tried to take advantage of her. But Jesus spoke with her and dignified her. In the same way, he touched people with skin diseases (Matthew 8:3) and made friends with foreigners (Luke 17:16). As I meditate on these stories and soak up his life, it changes the way I view and interact with people.

In addition to revealing God, the Bible also reveals what he thinks of us, which is important in a relationship. As we learn how he sees us, it changes how we see ourselves.

WHAT HE THINKS ABOUT US

The Bible is the one place we can see God's thoughts and opinions in a tangible form. It is a good idea to read what God says about us. We can use these truths to refute lies the enemy tells us. To give a short list, we are rooted and built up (Colossians 2:7), spiritually clean (Colossians 2:11), given a spirit of power (2 Timothy 1:7), raised and seated next to God (Ephesians 2:6), set apart and called a brother or sister of Jesus (Hebrews 2:11), and sealed by God (2 Corinthians 1:22). In addition to all that, we are children of God (John 1:12), the light of the world (Matthew 5:14), the dwelling place of God (1 Corinthians 3:16), and the list goes on.

You may find it helpful to insert your own name into a passage to make it more real. Greg Boyd suggests writing out scripture as personal truth rather than general truth.[1] We need to realize it is not just an old book. It is speaking to us. God's word is alive (Hebrews 4:12). The Bible gives us concrete ideas about who God is, especially as we learn who Jesus is. It also reveals what he thinks and feels about us. It is a steady framework. But he is not just a person from the past we can learn about. We can know him personally, in the present tense. He wants to interact with us.

PRAYER: A REAL-TIME CONVERSATION

Prayer is a real-time conversation. This means it involves talking and listening to God. While talking is important, it is only part of the process. We need to realize that God still speaks and he has much to tell us.

BE FREE

Jesus said that when we pray we don't need to use many words, and also that we shouldn't pray for the purpose of gaining attention from people. Instead, he instructed us to find a quiet place and offer simple words (Matthew 6:5–7). It is also important that we are raw and honest with God. In fact, the name given to God's people was Israel, which means "God contended." It is a combination of the words for "God" and "wrestle." The name was first given to Jacob, who literally fought with God. God wants us to be real with him. He wants us to tell him what is on our minds.

Talking to God can and should take many forms. I've yelled into my windshield at certain times and at other times, I've laid on my face crying into the carpet. Once, before I fell asleep, I simply asked God to do surgery on me. I asked him to remove the dead stuff while I was under. Prayer is personal, not ceremonial. Having said that, there is a weight to prayer. It is an actual interaction with the God of Heaven. The first time Moses talked to God, he took off his shoes (Exodus 3:5).

It is good and important that we bring our stuff to God. We can ask for power, for help, for rescue in the midst of struggle. John Eldredge calls these "cry of the heart" prayers. We need to be careful, however, that we are not just seeking results in place of the relationship.

God calls us his friends and his children (John 15:15, Romans 8:16). When I was young, I had a friend in the neighborhood who had a Nintendo. Anytime I went to his house, that was all I wanted to do. Looking back, I wonder if he felt like I only wanted to be his friend so I could use his stuff. And we've all heard about the estranged son or daughter who disappears until the parents die and it is time to collect on the estate. But this is not the kind of relationship God wants with us. The goal is a real relationship, which means that dialogue is vital.

MY SHEEP HEAR MY VOICE

Learning to hear from God can seem more difficult than learning to talk to him. There are a few reasons for this. First, God doesn't generally speak in an audible voice (although examples are found both in the Bible and in the personal testimonies of Jesus' followers). Second, many people don't believe God still speaks—at least not to them personally. The good news is that God does speak, and we can learn to hear him.

Genesis teaches that God made the universe with words. And in the beginning of John's gospel, Jesus is called "the Word," or "logos," which is the expression of thought. He is literally the expression of God in the world (John 1:1–3). Furthermore, Jesus said that he would speak and his sheep would hear and know his voice (John 10:27). Finally, Jesus explained he would send his Spirit to remind us of everything he said (John 14:26). God has always spoken, and he still speaks.

Learning to hear God's voice is a process. It is helpful to start with the mechanics of how it works. A great deal of variety and mystery surrounds hearing the voice of God, but I want to offer something practical and concrete to help this process. To do that, we need to think back to the discussion in Chapter 2 about our minds. Remember, we think in images. At all times, even when we are asleep, we have movies playing in our heads. These images often come from us or from things we've experienced. But they can also come from other places. Many of the destructive pictures come from Satan. But the Holy Spirit also uses pictures to speak to us. This can happen when we are awake or asleep. The Bible calls these pictures visions and dreams. The prophet Joel said that God would pour out his Spirit on all people and they would dream dreams and see visions (Joel 2:28). In the book of Acts, Peter confirmed that the pouring out of the Spirit has already begun (Acts 2:17).

In addition to the pictures we play, we also "hear" words. When I say "hear," I am referring to impressions rather than audible sounds. This hearing is what we do when we talk to ourselves in our minds. Like the images, these words often come from us, but they can also come from other sources. The lying words we hear come from the Enemy and the true words come from the God.

I recognize it may be a new idea for some. But we have a mind, and we are made in the image of God (Genesis 1:27). This means that God also has a mind. And if he has a mind, he must have thoughts. The

BE FREE

Bible says his thoughts are different than ours (Isaiah 55:8) and that his thoughts outnumber the grains of sand (Psalm 139:17–18). If the Holy Spirit lives in us, it makes sense that he would have the ability to prompt and direct our thinking with his thinking.

Talking about hearing God could activate a nerve for some. Many people have done horrific things and claimed God told them to. But there is a safeguard against this. Jesus said we would know things by their fruit (Matthew 7:16). As we learn to listen for God's voice, we can test what we hear against what we know of God from the Bible. The Holy Spirit will not contradict himself. Revelation from the Holy Spirit should illuminate and help us better understand the Bible—not contradict or change it.

The next thing is to simply start practicing by asking God questions when praying. This really isn't much different from how we learned to hear and understand human voices—we logged a lot of hours listening. Because it can be difficult to know where to start, I would like to offer a simple framework for prayer that can help guide the conversation. I should clarify that I didn't come up with this outline—Jesus did.

Jesus' disciples once came to him and said, "Teach us to pray" (Luke 11:1). In response, he offered this simple prayer (which is also found in Matthew).

> Our Father in heaven,
> hallowed be your name.
> Your kingdom come.
> Your will be done,
> on earth as it is in heaven.
> Give us this day our daily bread.
> And forgive us our debts,
> as we also have forgiven our debtors.
> And do not bring us to the time of trial,
> but rescue us from the evil one.
> —Matthew 6:9–13

SITTING ON A SONG

I love the simplicity of this prayer. It is the perfect place to start in our search for freedom. We begin by remembering that God is powerful and able to free us (hallowed be your name) but also that he is our good Father, which means he is willing to save us (Our Father in heaven). Next, we are confirming our choice to yield our independence to God (Your kingdom come, Your will be done). Directly from that place of yielding flows our decision to come to him as children with a trust that he will fill us (give us this day our daily bread). Then we declare we are dead to sin by bringing our past sin and brokenness to God (forgive us our debts, as we also have forgiven our debtors). We end by taking our place in Jesus and the victory he has already won over sin, Satan, and death (do not bring us to the time of trial, but rescue us from the evil one).

Now I would like to share with you a prayer I wrote that is based on the framework, but also takes into account the ideas that prayer is personal and that it can be treated as a conversation. I've recorded my questions in *italics* and when praying this prayer, I would pause after each question to listen.

> Father, Son, and Holy Spirit, you are powerful and good. You are not angry or indifferent toward me. Because of your love, you intervened to break me out of prison.
>
> I choose to give up my independence, and I acknowledge that you are the king and I'm not. I yield my heart to you and choose to run all my decisions through you. I yield my mind to you and ask for a supernatural filter for my thoughts, so I can hear your voice. And I yield my body to you. I give you the work of my hands and ask to be an apprentice under you. I trust you with my daily needs and I ask for you to fill me with your life. Please be my food.

I count myself dead to sin and I refuse to grasp for idols and cling to my old attachments. I also choose to forgive those who have sinned against me and contributed to my brokenness. *Will you reveal to me the things I still need to let go of? Also, will you show me if there are people I need to forgive and even bless?*

I also count myself alive to you, God. I know that I've been resurrected with you and choose to participate in the new reality you offer. Please heal my broken places, and also please give me your righteousness in exchange for my unrighteousness. *Is there anything else you would like me to trade in so I can receive what you are offering? (receive patience in exchange for anger, receive boldness in place of fear, etc.)*

Finally, I declare that you have taken back all authority from the accuser and you include me in that authority as your child. I take my place in your covering. You are my armor. In your name I bring your kingdom of light against the kingdom of darkness in my life and against all the tricks and lies of the devil. *Are there any lies that I am believing about you and about myself (or others)?* Show me the truth with which to destroy those lies.

While I hope this example will provide inspiration and direction, I want to make this idea of conversational prayer as accessible as I can. The best way to do that is to share with you a real-life example of a conversation with God about a particular area of struggle. We will call it a case study in prayer. As I share this, I ask you to keep an open mind. When we hear other people's stories about hearing from God, there is a temptation to either dismiss them because we've seen abuses in this area or to become discouraged because we don't think it is available to us. Neither are helpful. It is possible to genuinely hear from God, and it is available to everyone.

A CASE STUDY IN PRAYER

Recently I was in the middle of a struggle with my attachment to food (and sugar, more specifically). I was recognizing that I'd fallen into a pattern of over-consumption, and I was using sugar like a drug rather than opening myself to be filled by the Comforter. As I was praying about this, I asked the Holy Spirit if there was a deeper layer to this struggle, which there often is.

I heard one simple word in response: fear. Then in my mind I began to replay what had been happening over the past few weeks. My family was in the middle of a very difficult financial situation. I was feeling vastly overwhelmed by this and had been returning to food as a refuge.

As I kept praying, I sensed that the issue of fear wasn't just related to the current situation, but it was deeper. Then God brought back a memory from middle school. I was at football practice and the coach asked for a volunteer to play quarterback. I jumped in, but my lack of experience quickly revealed itself. I positioned myself several feet behind the center, not realizing I was supposed to place my hands between his legs to receive the snap. The coach quickly rebuked me, and my teammates began to laugh. While the memory may seem unrelated, it was actually the perfect picture of my battle with fear. For as long as I can remember, I have felt unqualified to handle difficult situations and have doubted my ability to lead. This lack of confidence followed me into adulthood and was magnified with the realization that I was responsible for other people. The result was that any time I was faced with a trial, I would fly into fear.

I needed to not only let go of my attachment to food, but also to repent of my fear because I recognized it was taking me into a place of independence from God. I also had to choose to forgive the coach and other players for mocking me. Not because they will ever know, but because unforgiveness prevents the broken places from healing.

While this was all helpful, it was only part of the process. The next thing was to open myself up to resurrection. I began to ask for his life to fill me. I asked for him to be my Comforter in place of food and asked him to give me faith in place of fear. I also invited his healing over the brokenness that had contributed to my sin.

He gave me another image at this point. I saw a kid wearing adult clothes (which was exactly how I felt). But then the kid grew into a man and the clothes began to fit. Then a memory came back to me of playing football in the yard with my sons. I was the man, but I was also the boy playing with his father. There was immense healing in this.

Finally, I took my place in Jesus' authority and asked the Holy Spirit to reveal any lies I was believing that needed to be replaced with truth. Ultimately, I was harboring the thought that my family would end up in serious trouble because I could not support them well enough. He reminded me that he provides for birds, and that I can do all things through him.

I mentioned earlier that God also speaks to us in dreams. A few nights after I was praying about all this, I had a dream. A van had rolled into a lake and was starting to sink. I saw myself wading into the water and then lifting the vehicle and carrying it to the shore. Then I realized my family was inside. It sounds a bit a crazy, I'll admit. But when I woke up, I asked for interpretation. It seemed pretty clear. Like I said, I can do all things through Christ who strengthens me (Philippians 4:13).

THINGS NOT SEEN

The takeaway from all this is that it is helpful to ask questions as we pray. Then we simply need to pay attention to words and images that come to mind. I will warn that as you begin to do this, there can be a tendency to doubt the process. One thing I struggled with a lot at first was the concern that I was just making this stuff up. How do I know, I wondered, if it is actually God or just my imagination?

Here is the good news, even if some of the words and images you begin to observe are coming from your mind, it does not invalidate them. We are not engaging in wishful thinking or make-believe. We are simply beginning to practice aligning our minds with what God has already said to be true. God says that we've been set free and we are part of the new creation. Our job is to believe what God says. And our belief can start with a choice to enter into God's way of seeing things. This applies to the past and the future.

Our memories are "re-presentations" that still send us messages about who we are. Many of us are filled with guilt over the things we've done and pain from things done to us. But God can redeem and heal our memories. Obviously, it doesn't change the past, but it can change the message of our past.[2] Jesus can begin to heal our identities as we envision him being present in the memories. This is because he was there—we just didn't know it. John Eldredge calls this process "sanctifying the past."[3]

It is also possible to see ourselves in future situations—the same way an athlete may run a mental race before approaching the line. Paul said that "faith is the assurance of things hoped for, the conviction of things not seen (Hebrews 11:1). We can envision the rehabilitated version of ourselves and fix our minds on that. Again, it is not fantasy, it is aligning with the truth. We are deciding to see ourselves the way God sees us, and it has the potential to change our actions.

Reading the Bible to know Jesus and engaging in conversational prayer are vital to our relationship with God. But we must go further. To continue to receive more of God's life and therefore freedom, we have to wade out to the point where we can no longer touch the bottom.

WORSHIP: BECOMING A LIVING SACRIFICE

God is already offering us his presence. He promised he would never leave or forsake us (Hebrews 13:5, Deuteronomy 31:6). Jesus also said that the Spirit is given without measure (John 3:34). The offer for more of God is there, always available to us. But sometimes we don't experience more of God because we have areas that we've not yielded to make space for him to enter. The purpose of worship is to fully surrender every remnant of control and to open every last room of the house to give God full access. Then his presence can rush in. This is what Paul meant when he instructed us to offer ourselves as living sacrifices to God as our spiritual form of worship (Romans 12:1).

We've spent much of this book talking about yielding our lives back to God, but this is the full measure. There is no turning back. For this reason, it can feel overwhelming and risky at first. But remember, we've already been opening ourselves up to something. We've seen how we lost all control in our pursuit of life apart from God. All of our sin was actually a form of worship. We were just worshiping the wrong thing. This is why turning our worship back to God is the best antidote for sin. As we become more filled with his presence, it flushes out everything else. In fact, God will continue to fill us to overflow.

Isaiah said that the train of God's robe fills the temple (Isaiah 6:1). And Paul said that our bodies are a temple for the Holy Spirit (1 Corinthians 6:19). This means God can fill us beyond capacity. And this is the whole point. It is not just that we would have his life flowing in us, but that it would spill out and land on the world around us. The more we give away, the more he will fill us. This is what Jesus was referring to when he said he could give "a spring of water gushing up to eternal life" (John 4:14).

When we consider all this, it becomes clear that the only true risk is to withhold our worship and allow the remnants of the old life to remain. In addition to being an act of full surrender, worship is also an expression of gratitude for everything God has done and who God is.

ENTHRONED ON PRAISES

After Mary learned she would be giving birth to Jesus, she went to visit her cousin Elizabeth. When Elizabeth saw her, she began to bless her and then Mary began to praise God. She said,

> My soul magnifies the Lord, and my spirit rejoices in God my Savior, for he has looked with favor on the lowliness of his servant . . . for the mighty one has done great things for me . . . he has brought down the powerful from their thrones, he has lifted up the

> lowly; he has filled the hungry with good things.
> —Luke 1:46–53

When confronted with the reality of who God is, Mary simply began to thank him and exalt him. In the gospel of Luke, a woman fell at Jesus' feet and began to cry. Then she wiped his feet clean with her hair (Luke 7:38). In the presence of Jesus' mercy and goodness, the only thing she could think to do was worship. God's strength also evokes worship. This is the reason people tried to worship Paul. They saw him heal a man and thought he was a god (Acts 14:8–18). Paul quickly corrected them, but the point remains—when we truly begin to encounter the power of the Holy Spirit, worship is the only response that makes any sense.

This type of worship reinforces our trust in God. Everything God has done in the past displays his character. And God does not change (Malachi 3:6, James 1:17). As we remember what he has done in the past, we can be assured about what he will do in the future. This is why Isaiah told the barren one to sing (Isaiah 54:1). The metaphor is encouraging us to thank God even before our current situation has been resolved because we know God is with us and for us. The twenty-second Psalm begins with an expression of feeling forsaken by God, but then turns a sharp corner to praise. The psalmist wrote, "Yet you are holy, enthroned on the praises of Israel. In you our ancestors trusted; they trusted and you delivered them." (Psalm 22:3–4). The reason for the shift was a decision to remember what God has done so as to foster trust in who God is.

We are simply proclaiming what we already know to be true about God. He has already won our freedom and is now in the process of restoring all things. And we are a part of that restoration. Remembering this will keep us far from deception and will also give way to hope. I was sitting at the table the other day with my family and the Holy Spirit prompted the thought that no matter how much of God we are experiencing now, there is always more available. This means we can always live in anticipation. And when we stay in the goodness of God, it will keep our hearts open to receiving

BE FREE

more of the life and freedom he is offering.

A while back, my wife and I were participating in a worship service with several hundred people. As we started to sing, I decided to enter a place of gratitude for all God has done. Something tangible began to shift in me almost immediately. There were people around the room waving flags, which was a new experience for me. If I am honest, there was a time when I may have responded with judgment. But instead, I was filled with hope. I felt I was part of a celebration that was honoring the one who is worthier than any other. Then suddenly, I began to weep. I could hardly sing the rest of the time. I started to check my pockets for Kleenex. This was not normal for me, either. This whole letting go of control has been one of the hardest things for me. But for possibly the first time in my life, worship did feel not forced, it was the only thing that made sense. I was crying because of joy.

I've been careful not to directly equate worship with music because they are not the same thing. As we've seen worship is not primarily the external things we do. It is the willingness to yield to God's presence and to express gratitude for who he is. The external expressions of worship are a natural response to the internal posture. Having said that, music is a very common way to express worship. Part of the reason is because music, like other forms of art, can connect us to realities beyond our immediate comprehension. For this reason, I'd like to just say a few words about music specifically.

FAMILY BAND

While music is a powerful expression of worship, the effectiveness of our worship is not based on our talents or abilities—musical or otherwise. People see outward appearances, but God sees the heart (1 Samuel 16:7). The only requirement is that we show up. Worship is not passive. We have to let go and allow joy to overwhelm us.

My aunt teaches piano. She said she has two students who have strong technical skill. They can follow written music and are very methodical. But she told me she is trying to teach them to play in the

Spirit. She is encouraging them to improvise and create. In other words, she is asking them to risk mistakes in order to make something new.

For me, the most beautiful illustration of worship expressed through music comes from my family. One day we were in church, and I looked over at my daughter, Ellie. She was dancing to the music like there was no one in the room. Our two youngest sons, JJ and Ezra, are always picking up the ukulele (which they think is a guitar) to play improvised songs without any reservations. Our son Noah is constantly drumming. Rhythms just roll off his fingers like they are leaving without his permission. And our oldest, Sam, has started writing lyrics to his own rap songs about the battle between good and evil and about Jesus' victory over death. And the family band culminates with my wife and I singing old songs from the camp where we met. What I love about the music my family makes is the inhibition and joy of it all. Surrender and gratitude open the door wide for God's presence to enter.

PRACTICING PRESENCE OF GOD

It is easy to think of reading the Bible, prayer, and worship as tasks. And honestly, it will feel that way at times. The same thing is true in marriage. We often have to make choices to do things that will build a relationship even if we don't always feel the emotion.

The beauty is that once we make the choice, the life follows. As we begin to experience the freedom that comes from walking with God, we won't want to turn back. When Jesus asked Peter if he wanted to leave, he said, "Lord, to whom can we go? You have the words of eternal life" (John 6:68).

Eventually these practices will no longer be things we start and stop, but things that are mixed up with the reality of our lives. An old saint named Brother Lawrence called this "practicing the presence of God." He talked about continually dwelling in God's presence like it was the house he lived in.[4] It is like David, who said, "I keep the LORD always before me" (Psalm 16:8).

God's words become like our food, and we can understand what

BE FREE

Jesus meant in the wilderness about not needing bread. We can also understand what he meant when he talked about living water that would prevent us from getting thirsty again (John 4:14). Proverbs says that his words are healing and life (Proverbs 4:20–22).

There was an Old Testament command to bind the scripture to the hand and forehead (Deuteronomy 6:8). Some of God's people took it literally as a way of keeping the words on their minds. Though I am not sure the instruction was meant to be taken literally, it is a powerful symbol. And I once heard of a man who started every prayer with the words "Now, Lord," as though he was picking up where he left off in an open-ended, continuous conversation. Then there are those people who are always humming, or people like my wife who will wake up in the middle of the night to watch a meteor shower and quietly worship the one who caused it.

When we learn to live in this place, independence from God begins to seem like a foolish idea. As we get more and more life from him, we don't need to go looking in other places and freedom becomes our reality.

This is all beautiful and good and real. The things we've discussed in this chapter are vital to our lives and our freedom. However, there is still something very important we have not addressed. The reality is, we can't see God the way we can see a person sitting next to us (at least not yet). But we long for that level of presence. It seems like a requirement for real unity. And maybe it is. Thankfully, God made a way for even this to happen.

See, he actually does have a body we can see and hear and touch. His body is called the church. And it is through this body that everything else we've talked about becomes a more tangible reality.

CHAPTER 11

A BODY THAT CAN'T BE KILLED
LOVE LEADS US INTO FREEDOM

CANYONS AND CABINS

If you lived alone in an empty canyon, solitude and silence would be normative, and it would not be hard to fast due to a lack of options. You could read the Bible by sun and firelight, and pray without stopping. You could open your mouth and let your voice fly off the walls of the canyon in worship. These things would all bring you into closer relationship with Jesus, but there would still be something vital missing.

I was once at a cabin for a few days. I was not only separated from family, but from all human interaction. There was still visible life around me. In addition to all the plants and trees, I spent the weekend with two horses and a bunch of cows. There were also squirrels, birds, and bugs. It didn't take long for me to begin to feel lonely. I could see why no suitable partner was found in the animals (Genesis 2:20).

We looked before at the importance of solitude as a discipline, and it is important—but it is not meant to be a lifestyle. It is a tool to be used for periods of time, and then we need to return to relationships. One of the harshest punishments that can be imposed on a prisoner is solitary confinement. As God said in the beginning, it is not good for us to be alone (Genesis 2:18).

We need each other. Not just to make it through life but to fully experience the presence of Jesus, and therefore, find our freedom.

GOD'S SPIRIT DWELLS IN HIS BODY, THE CHURCH

In the Incarnation, something happened that is beyond our comprehension. The fullness of God's Spirit dwelled in a single, human body

BE FREE

(Colossians 2:9). Before he died, Jesus promised his friends he would send this same Spirit to help them (John 14:16). Then after Jesus had gone back to the Father, the fire of his Spirit fell on his followers at Pentecost (Acts 2:3).

We've talked about his Spirit entering us individually. This is a beautiful reality, but there is more. The idea here is that we can also become a place for his Spirit to dwell collectively. Jesus said that where two or three are gathered in his name, he will be there (Matthew 18:20). Paul wrote that we are being "built together spiritually into a dwelling place for God" (Ephesians 2:22). He wasn't talking about a building made with stone or metal. The other morning, I walked into the church where I work, before anyone else was there. It was still dark outside. It felt empty and lonely. There was a tangible difference from when the place is filled with people. This is because God's Spirit dwells in us. That is why Paul also called us the body of Christ (1 Corinthians 12:27).

Now, instead of the Spirit of God dwelling in one human body, it dwells in billions of bodies, making a giant body with long arms that can wrap around the entire world. It is a body so big that it can't be killed.

The enemy has tried to kill this body. Through his deception he has often turned the hearts of kings and rulers against Christians. Many in power have become fixed on executing this body. Almost all the apostles were killed, and the early church lived and grew under the same threat. The attacks have continued throughout the history of the church, but the body only continues to grow. Missionary Gladys Aylward spent her life in China during the rise of communism. Near the end of her life, she watched as one of the students she had instructed was asked to renounce Jesus in the middle of the town square. She refused and was beheaded for it. Instead of fleeing, two hundred more students stood up and followed her to heaven.[1] As I said, this is a body that can't be killed.

It is when we are connected to this body that we tap into the most powerful current of God's strength and life. His power flows forcefully through the veins of his body. The other night I heard a choir singing as I was picking up my kids. Their voices vibrated through my body. There is a power found in the collective that does not exist in an individual alone. Through this body we can experience the tangible power of God to walk out of our prisons. There are many reasons why this is true.

STRENGTH IN NUMBERS

It is a simple fact that there is strength in numbers. Musician Rich Mullins once told a story about his struggle to stay pure. Rich was a single guy, and for a while he traveled alone doing shows. He often felt assaulted by temptation, especially at night in the hotels. He was talking to a friend about it, and the man gave him a simple response. He told him that he wasn't struggling because he was bad, but because none of us are supposed to do this alone.

I heard a different musician talking once about trying to break free from smoking. The last time he decided to quit, he'd gone a few days and the craving was overpowering him. He started walking late at night to find a gas station. When he got to the store, he saw an old man smoking outside. He started talking to the man and found out he had lung cancer and was dying. The man hadn't seen his kids in a while, so he was driving his motorcycle across to the country to visit them before the cancer finished him off. This musician said he hadn't touched a cigarette since that night.

This is the reason support groups are so powerful. Alcoholics Anonymous is known not just for its twelve-step structure, but for the intentional "social arrangements in which they are concretely embodied."[2] In other words, it is a place where people who have faced the same demons can walk away together. Two are better than one, for if one falls, the other can lift him up (Ecclesiastes 4:9–10).

To give a personal example, I have referred to my struggle with food, specifically sugar, several times. It is something that has often had a strong, squeezing hold; a place I go for comfort apart from God. Through much of the process of writing this book, I have felt

BE FREE

conflicted. I was writing about freedom but still felt deeply attached to this substance. I finally came to realize I could not get free from this on my own. Then, through Heather, God plowed me over with his grace (as he often does).

After taking our son to the doctor for headaches, my wife discovered a program called Whole30. It is a way of cooking and eating that eliminates processed sugars (and many other things) for thirty days. The idea is to starve what the authors call the "sugar dragon."[3]

Heather suggested we take on the challenge together as a family. So we cleaned out our pantry and fridge, did some shopping, and started on a Saturday morning. We made almost everything from scratch. My son, Noah, helped me make roasted red pepper sauce, which tasted amazing, although the pickled peppers looked like dead fish in a jar. JJ helped me squeeze fresh lime and lemon juice and slice vegetables. We learned the correct way to pan-fry steak and roast chicken without making meat shards. We even made a pizza crust out of cauliflower.

Over time, a peace started in my gut that moved to my fingertips and out through the soles of my feet. I began to feel stronger and our home began to change. We did it as a family, and they gave me strength.

AN AUDIBLE VOICE

God speaks through people. That may sound strange because we are imperfect. But if God didn't speak through imperfect people, there would not be a Bible. I heard a story about a preacher who used to go and teach in prisons. He would ask the inmates if God could use people who were guilty of murder. Then he would start ripping the pages out of the Bible that were recorded by murderers. Once you take out Moses, David, and Paul, there is a lot missing. Even Isaiah did not want to speak on behalf of God because he had unclean lips (Isaiah 6:5). But God purified him and used him anyway.

But why do we need people to speak? It is because the enemy wants to isolate us. Remember Jesus pursued the man who was imprisoned by demons and was living alone in the tombs.

He set the man free and then restored him to his community. Jesus told him to go back to his friends (Mark 5:1–20).

When we are cut off from other people, the Enemy can talk to us without much competition. Then it is easy for him to bring on the condemnation, temptation, and especially intimidation. We often need others to remind us of the truth. And it really helps if the voice is audible.

When I go to fear, Heather reminds me I can trust. When we were first entering into the financial crisis I mentioned earlier, I was talking to her on the phone and just giving way to fear. I told her I felt shaken. She then told me about how our kids had just been practicing reading Psalm 16:8, which says, "because he is at my right hand, I shall not be moved." Just in case it didn't take hold, I heard someone a few days later quote Hebrews 12:28: "since we are receiving a kingdom that cannot be shaken, let us give thanks . . ."

Other people can also provide loving correction, which leads to conviction. Paul said that we should teach and admonish one another in wisdom (Colossians 3:16). When I lose my patience, Heather calls me into my identity and reminds me of who I am in Jesus. The other day I was getting a bit short with my son Sam. Heather put her hand on my shoulder and simply said, "You are better than that, bud." God has often used my kids in the same way.

Once when Heather and I were arguing about something, it was Sam who stepped in with his hands raised and reminded us to speak nicely to each other. A little while later we were praying as a family, and our daughter shared a picture she had in her mind when our family argues. She said we were at a picnic, but then it started to rain and the grass got all wet and our sandwiches got soggy. It is hard not to receive correction from a six-year-old talking about soggy sandwiches.

Shortly after we got married, Heather and I moved to Norfolk, Virginia. We had no family around and knew no one. The isolation felt even greater because of where we lived. It was also common to hear our neighbors on the other side of the wall arguing and breaking things. I became very focused on my work, and we were struggling in our marriage. I was often cold to Heather and did not know how to love her well. Then we found George Harvey. He was an elderly counselor—a true sage. Peace radiated from him. We started talking to George, and he began to help me. He corrected me on many things, but I honestly never felt condemned. George was calling us into something better. He gave me what he called "velvet covered bricks." He was a man of grace and truth (John 1:17).

We do have to be a bit careful with this. When offering or receiving correction, it helps to have a relationship in place. It is not our job to correct people we don't even know and none of us like to receive a rebuke from a stranger. This only leads to judgment. For this reason, it is okay to be selective about whom we ask to speak over us and whom we are listening to. People say a lot of things that aren't from God. After all, the tongue does have the power of life and death in it (Proverbs 18:21). We have to discern what we are hearing and test things by their fruit.

Cautionary words aside, we need the voices of others to convict us because we are often deceived about our own stuff. If I am deceived, I won't likely be aware of it. That is the nature of deception. One afternoon I was driving home and saw a young man walking out onto a frozen lake. The problem was, the lake wasn't very frozen anymore. It was over forty degrees outside and had been for several days. There was open water and puddles all over the surface of the ice. The kid was shuffling out toward the middle of the lake with his head down and his hands in his pockets. He also had a large backpack over his shoulders. I turned around and pulled onto the side of the road. Then I ran through the brush and down to the edge of the water. Without thinking I yelled, "What are you doing? You shouldn't be out there!" The kid lifted his head, turned around, and walked back to shore, which surprised me. When he got back, I told him I was sorry to impose, but I thought he could have gotten himself killed, and I didn't want him to get hurt.

I believe everything I've told you so far. I know the truth, and yet there are still times freedom feels far away, and I forget the very words I am writing. We need other people to continue to remind us of the truth and yell to us from the shore. If we only live in our own heads,

A BODY THAT CAN'T BE KILLED

we are in trouble. We need intervention. In addition to speaking truth to each other, one of the best ways we can intervene is through prayer.

IF MY PEOPLE WILL PRAY

One of the Old Testament authors wrote, "If my people who are called by my name humble themselves, pray, seek my face, and turn from their wicked ways, then I will hear from heaven, and will forgive their sin and heal their land" (2 Chronicles 7:14). Notice the reference to "people." There is power when we pray together and pray on behalf of each other. Often when my kids are sleeping at night, I will place a hand on their back and pray protection and blessing over them. I like to think my prayers are covering them like a blanket. We need people to pray for us. It is also helpful when others will listen on our behalf. Sometimes it is easier to hear what God is saying to another person than it is to hear for ourselves. This is because we are a bit removed and there is less in the way.

Once I was sitting in an airport with my friend. He was recounting a nightmare that he'd had since he was a kid. In the dream, he was a young boy who was trapped in a castle in the middle of the jungle. There were these hooded monks who guarded him. They provided him with food and he believed they were protecting him from the wolves and panthers that lived in the jungle. But he also felt like he was their prisoner because he couldn't leave. If he tried to run, the animals would attack the monks and some would be killed. My friend believed he'd caused their death and felt guilt and shame over trying to escape. He also described an awareness of a wall in the jungle that was a further barrier to his freedom. He believed that even if he escaped the castle he would be trapped.

The other important piece of his story is that he often experienced large amounts of guilt—sometimes even over things that weren't his fault. After listening to his dream, we prayed. Almost immediately I had a strong sense that I was supposed to tell him the monks were not protecting him and he didn't have to stay in the castle. I sensed the Holy

Spirit saying that they were actually the ones keeping him in prison under the threat of guilt. I told him God could take him out of that place and even the wall was not high enough to stop him. We finished praying and the conversation ended with both of us laughing—him at his increased sense of freedom and me at his joy.

I've often been on other side of that scenario as well. My Aunt Lois has spent many early mornings praying for my family and me. She will often call to relay what God has spoken to her. Or she will write it down on notebook paper and mail it to us. She knows about my battle with fear and recently she called to offer a hopeful picture she was given in prayer. She saw Heather and I walking on unsteady ground that was sinking under our feet. But then the ground changed and it looked like we were walking on water that was firm like glass. After receiving the picture, my aunt sensed Jesus telling us to stand strong and trust him and stated he would turn the boulders in our path into sand. I knew the Holy Spirit was trying to bring me to a place of trust but having the prayer and words of my aunt strengthened my faith greatly. It really helps to hear it from someone else who walks with God and listens to his voice.

While all of this is good, there is at least one more reason we need other people and it is probably the most important. Relationships are necessary in order for us to give and receive love and love is the whole point of freedom.

THE PURPOSE OF FREEDOM IS LOVE

Jesus was once asked what was the greatest commandment. He responded by saying, "'You shall love the Lord your God with all your heart, and with all your soul, and with all your mind.' This is the greatest and first commandment. And a second is like it: 'You shall love your neighbor as yourself'" (Matthew 22:36–39). Love God and love others. According to Jesus, love is the reason we are here. Paul confirmed this when he said that if we don't love, we have nothing (1 Corinthians 13:1–3). And James said that we need to be more than hearers of the word, we need to do what it says (James 1:22).

We can choose to practice love. And practicing love forces us to look outward and thus wages war on sin, which is inherently self-focused. When we love someone else by serving him or her, it takes us outside of ourselves. Sin happens in the first place because of our chronic, inward focus. If we stare consistently at our own wants, we become consumed with self and it keeps us in prison. The antidote is to love and serve each other. As we practice love, we become freer. So how do we practice love?

The first thing to do is simply find something you can do for someone else. I know a man who was bound by alcohol most his life. It was an addiction he'd inherited from his father. When drinking almost killed him, the man decided to stop. He picked up an old hobby of building musical instruments, like guitars. I know because he made one for me. I believe this outward focus is part of what helps him stay free.

Once I was tied up in my own head because I wanted something to happen that wasn't. As I was railing, I got a text saying a family member was in a life-threatening surgery. My priorities quickly became clear, and I began to pray for this person. The issues I thought were so important just a second before were suddenly gone. Focusing on someone else takes us outside of ourselves and into freedom.

The next thing to do is to remember we are part of a collective and that even our individual choices impact other people. I carry my wife and kids with me in my mind when I am away from them. As I've mentioned, the world assaults us with sensual images, and thinking of my family helps me remember how important it is to win the fight. I've also noticed my sons respond to their mother the way they see me respond. This awareness helps me remember what is at stake and what I am fighting to stay free for. It easy for me to be concerned for the well-being of my family because they are close to me. But this concern can spread outside my circle if I am willing to look at people the way God sees them, which leads to the next point.

One of the best ways to help me practice loving another person is to remember that Jesus considered that person worth dying for. God has assigned immense worth to people and if we will align ourselves with

BE FREE

that mind-set, it will change how we treat people. Take pornography as an example. The thing that allows anyone to use another person sexually (whether in the flesh or in the mind) is a failure to assign worth and dignity to that person. I once saw a study that showed fathers who help care for their infant children (feeding and holding, for example) rarely ever abuse them sexually.[4] The choice to start seeing people as people can bring immense freedom.

The choice to assign worth to people also helps us love even when someone is being unloving to us. The other day one of our kids was having a difficult time and was talking to my wife and me in an extremely rude tone. I was about to offer a stern rebuke but Heather called our son into the kitchen and just wrapped her arms around him. He softened in her arms and immediately turned around.

The powerful thing is that this kind of love not only helps us, it has the power to change the recipient. Paul said that God's kindness leads to repentance (Romans 2:4) and we have the ability to be a vessel of God's kindness. Our choice to love can change the world because love breeds more love. Jesus said I've washed your feet now you wash one another's feet (John 13:14). Love spreads.

DAVE'S CAR

Several years ago, my friend Dave learned about a difficult situation my family was in. I had to drive across a couple of states to pick up Heather and the kids. They'd gotten a ride up with family for a funeral, and I couldn't go. I needed to get them to bring them home. The problem was, our car wasn't very reliable. My friend Dave told me to take his car and also gave me $100 for gas. The experience led me to a question. Did Dave loan me his car because he did not have a struggle with materialism. Or, was Dave free from materialism because he made a practice of loaning his car to people? The answer is yes . . . to both questions.

See, there is a beautiful paradox to all of this. The more we practice love, the more free we become. The more free we become, the easier it is to love.

Love abounds among people who are free. This is because free people look up and out instead of in. Because we are pouring out, there is more room for God to fill us. And the more God fills us, the more we have to give. As May says, the freer we become, the "less self-preoccupied" we are.[5] This means the more we practice, the easier it gets. Eventually, we won't even feel like we have to choose love. It will come naturally and build into a momentum that is unstoppable. We can get caught up into a force that is far stronger than our sin ever was.

This life of freedom is available. Nothing has the power to stop us from entering into it. And once we do, we will experience a process of ever-increasing freedom.

CHAPTER 12

NOT AS FREE AS I'M GONNA BE
PROGRESS VS. PERFECTION

GET UP SEVEN TIMES

I used to have dreams I was running across mountain terrain. In the dreams, I could jump over hills and rivers—like I was on the moon. My strides wouldn't even really touch the ground. I just pushed myself through the air.

Once when I was actually in the mountains, I decided to test the dream. I started running along a creek. I was navigating tree roots and rocks when I came to a bridge. It looked wet, but that wasn't a concern for a man who could fly. I stepped on to the bridge and slipped. My body came down directly on my right knee, and I almost fell into the water. Instant pain pulsed through my leg and fear jumped on me.

The year before, I'd broken that same knee. It was a fluke injury. My feet were planted in a parking lot, and I twisted my upper body to speak to a friend. I felt something break loose and my leg gave out. Within a few days, I noticed a bump under the skin on the side of my knee. I touched it, and it moved. I limped around for several weeks out of avoidance. Then one day I went outside to play with my kids. When I stood up, my knee locked at a ninety-degree angle. The MRI showed two broken pieces. This led to two surgeries and crutches for almost a year. It was madness. Heather had to carry the weight of the family. I couldn't hold my daughter's hand or pick her up. I couldn't play with the boys. At one of the low points, my crutches came out from under me on an icy patch near the mailbox. Laying on my back, I looked up and argued with heaven.

So, back to the mountain. When I fell, a fear came over me. I thought I was back to the beginning. I believed I had undone the last surgery with the force of the fall. But then a saving thought landed in my mind. I heard the Father say, "Get up and keep running, Son." I stood up, limped two steps, and then the pain left almost instantly. I ran the rest of the way.

As you work through this process of finding freedom, it is possible you will fall on a wet bridge. You may even fall in an area where you thought you were already free. We need to know that a fall doesn't mean the end. Paul said we may be struck down but we are not destroyed (2 Corinthians 4:9). My friend Neal says we should realize the road we are on has ditches on both sides. Our old attachments and sins are not somewhere back in the distance, they are within reach on either side, so our job is to stay on the path. This is encouraging because if we stumble and choose sin, it doesn't mean we've gone backward, it just means we veered. All progress is not lost, we just need to get back up. As the ancient author wrote, "though [the righteous] fall seven times, they will rise again" (Proverbs 24:16). Then we must keep moving forward. And Paul told us to run in such a way to win the race (1 Corinthians 9:24). Finally, the old preacher A. W. Tozer advised us to follow hard after God.[1] Our hope for freedom is fully contingent on following Jesus and clinging to him.

We also need to remember that he is there to help us stand back up. John wrote that if we sin, we have an advocate (1 John 2:1). We may not have the power, but he does. Our job is to offer whatever we have and let him infuse it with his power. In the face of a hungry crowd, Jesus asked the disciples to tell him what they had instead of focusing on what they didn't have. They gave him five loaves of bread and two fish. He fed thousands (John 6:1–14).

The defeat comes if we stay on the ground or if we turn around and run the other way. Remember, our enemy does not want us to be free. It is a substantial threat to the kingdom of darkness when a son or daughter begins to exercise his or her freedom. He will try to convince us to stay down or to stop the pursuit of God. For this reason, we need to stay on guard as we contend for freedom.

In the Old Testament, Nehemiah led the people back to Jerusalem after their exile. The walls of the city were destroyed, and his job was to direct the rebuilding effort. Nehemiah instructed the people never

NOT AS FREE AS I'M GONNA BE

to take off their weapons (Nehemiah 4:23). We, too, must keep our weapon close. Our weapon is the truth.

The repeated cry of this book has been freedom found in Jesus. We've looked at the reality of our freedom, but also at the process of becoming free.

A PROCESS THAT TAKES TIME

Many of us have spent a long time in prison. This means the process toward freedom may also take some time. There will be breakthroughs that seem to happen quickly. But much of the journey takes longer. My friend Morgan says we need to measure our life in decades.

It reminds me of the time I came home one winter night after work. When I opened the car door, the cold bit my fingers. The skin on my hands always cracks in the winter. As I walked around the front of the car, I felt heat seeping out from the engine.

I laid my hands on the hood like I was praying for healing. The warm metal began to bring blood back to my hands. As I turned to go in, my daughter Ellie came running toward me. She reached my legs, cranked her neck back, and held up a mitten. It was hers. She told me to put it on because my hands were cold. I took the mitten from her and slid it onto my hand. It covered three of my fingers down to the first knuckle.

BE FREE

This is how the Holy Spirit brings us back to life, I think. The Spirit is a fire that restores the heat we lost. But the restoration is a process. The feeling comes back to our fingers gradually. The good news is it gets easier. The more freedom we taste and the more we receive the life of God, the less we need our old ways. If the progress seems quiet or slow to start, don't be discouraged. The momentum builds, and the initial flame will ignite into a raging fire within us.

I remember my friend telling me about how he was making extra payments on his house to cut away at his mortgage. He talked about how he and his wife were freer with each payment they made. Musician Jonathan David Helser once said to a group of worshipers, "You are not as free as you're gonna be." At each stage, we know there is even more available. This means the goal is to make progress.

PROGRESS TOWARD PERFECTION

Paul said when he was a child he thought like a child, but as he grew he put the ways of childhood behind him (1 Corinthians 13:11). He also talked about people still needing milk instead of solid food, the implication being we should graduate to eating meat (metaphorically speaking) (1 Corinthians 3:2). Finally, he hoped we would grow up in every way into him who is the head (Ephesians 4:15). He was talking about making progress.

But Paul also acknowledged that we are not yet perfect. He said there will come a day when we will be fully transformed into the likeness of Jesus as we move from one degree of glory to another (2 Corinthians 3:18). Graham Cooke calls it receiving upgrades. And for now, we see in a dim mirror, but one day, we will see his face. For now, we know in part, but one day we will know fully (1 Corinthians 13:12).

The paradise we hope for will be a reality again. But we are not there yet. Not because God doesn't love us, but because God is inviting us into the restoration process. He is reinstating our original role of ruling with him. We helped break the world and God now wants to use us to help put it back together. The process is dignifying. Jesus told

Peter he would have a role in rebuilding the church and the gates of hell would not prevail against it (Matthew 16:18). In the same passage where Paul declared all things new, he also said that we've now been given the "ministry of reconciliation" so we can help reconcile the world to God (2 Corinthians 5:17–19). Paul also wrote,

> For by grace you have been saved through faith, and this is not your own doing; it is the gift of God—not the result of works, so that no one may boast. For we are what he has made us, created in Christ Jesus for good works, which God prepared beforehand to be our way of life.—Ephesians 2:8–10

What are the good works he has given us to do? Our work is to take part in the restoration. Our work is to walk with God as he leads us further into freedom and to help others do the same. It reminds me of the time I drove my family up a mountain . . .

PIKE'S PEAK

When I was a kid, we traveled as a family to Colorado Springs. I don't remember much of the trip, but I do remember riding up Pike's Peak on the cog railway. It is a small string of train cars that are pulled up the side of the mountain with cogwheels that move over a rack rail. Picture a couple of gears rotating over a long line of teeth. The ride was jarring, but it was also fun and probably the easiest way to get up the mountain—easy in the sense that it required little effort.

A few years ago, Heather and I took our kids back out to Colorado. We started to talk about making the trip up the mountain and something in me resisted the cog railway. At the same time, the thought of driving up the mountain scared me. I was caught in the tension of growth. I was no longer a child, and so I felt the need to take a risk. But I also knew that there were very few guardrails on the highway and almost no shoulder. And once you passed the timberline, there

BE FREE

weren't even trees to slow a vehicle from rolling down the mountain like a bolder. We decided to drive. I was in a state of fierce tension the entire trip.

However, once we reached the top, the fear got thin like the air. As we got out of the van I looked across the way and saw a train just finishing its climb. I began to feel the joy of progress—the satisfaction of pressing through fear and taking a risk. And I hadn't done it alone, probably would have never tried. Heather and the kids put on courage and stood there with me.

NOT AS FREE AS I'M GONNA BE

But I also saw something else on the top of Pike's Peak. There were people on bikes. I don't mean motorcycles, I mean they were pedaling up the side of the mountain. We'd seen them riding during our ascent. Then a thought was impressed on me that shocked me (I am still not sure if I believe it). The thought was, "You could do that some day." The Holy Spirit was trying to push me further. He was trying to help me fix my eyes on more progress, moving toward perfection.

While I am not sure when or how I will ever ride a bike to the top of a fourteen-thousand-foot peak, I do know that we follow a powerful God who loves us and who displays his strength in our weakness. And I also know I am not as free today as I'm gonna be. From what I know of God and what I've seen in others, so much more is available—I've barely scratched the surface. In fact, one day I will be so free I won't need a train or a van or a bike to climb a mountain. I will be able to run without even touching the ground.

And so will you.

APPENDIX A
GOD'S RESPONSE TO OUR SIN

Satan blinds and deceives the whole world (2 Corinthians 4:4)	Jesus came to restore the sight of the blind (Luke 4:18)
When we sin we become slaves to sin (John 8:34)	Jesus came to release prisoners and free captives (Luke 4:18)
Sin breaks the heart and results in death (Romans 6:23)	Jesus came to bind up the brokenhearted (Isaiah 61:1)

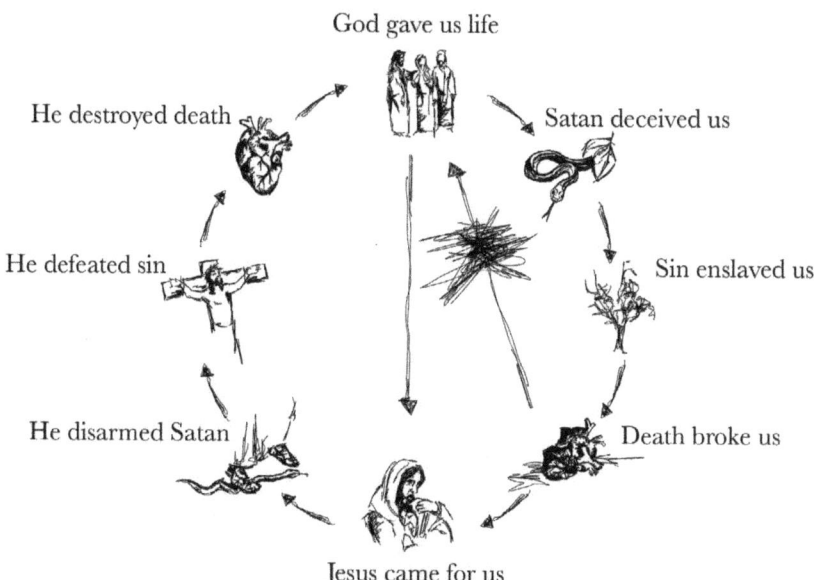

163

APPENDIX B
ADDITIONAL RESOURCES

I mentioned in the introduction that this book is intended to serve as a starting point in your journey to finding freedom. Below is a list of additional resources that have helped me in the pursuit of freedom.

- *Addiction and Grace* by Gerald G. May, M.D.
- *The Bondage Breaker* by Neil T. Anderson
- *The Pursuit of God* by A. W. Tozer
- *Seeing is Believing* by Gregory A. Boyd
- *The Spirit of the Disciplines* by Dallas Willard
- *This is Your Brain on Joy* by Dr. Earl Henslin
- *Free to Live* by John Eldredge

ACKNOWLEDGMENTS

Before any other, I have to acknowledge Jesus, the one who set me free. He deserves everything I have and is the one who gives me the ability and the reason to write.

There have been many times I have wanted to stop writing out of discouragement. My wife Heather is the reason I haven't. She believes this is what I am supposed to do and has sacrificed far more than I can explain in order to make a way for me to complete this book. I love her and I want to be a freer man because of her. She is beautiful in all ways.

Often while I was working on this book, one or more of my kids would run into the room to talk or to show me a piece of art they made or to just sit near me. I love them so much and they are a constant picture of what is available to us as children of God.

I have many talented friends who helped this process along and were all critical to the completion of the project. They are a strong example of how the body works, and I am grateful for them.

NOTES

Introduction
1. A. W. Tozer, *The Pursuit of God* (Lexington, KY: SoHo Books, 2010), 11.

Chapter 1
1. Dallas Willard, *Renovation of the Heart: Putting on the Character of Christ* (Colorado Springs: NavPress, 2002), 100.
2. C. S. Lewis, *The Screwtape Letters* (New York: HarperOne, 1942), 57.

Chapter 2
1. Dallas Willard, *Renovation of the Heart: Putting on the Character of Christ* (Colorado Springs: NavPress, 2002), 32–33.
2. C. S. Lewis, *Mere Christianity* (New York: Macmillan, 1943), 54.
3. Gerald G. May, M.D., *Addiction & Grace: Love and Spirituality in the Healing of Addictions* (New York: HarperOne, 1988), 112.
4. Willard, *Renovation of the Heart*, 40.
5. May, *Addiction & Grace*, 110.
6. Lewis, *Mere Christianity*, 54.
7. Willard, *Renovation of the Heart*, 35.
8. May, *Addiction & Grace*, 26–27.
9. Ibid., 14.
10. Damon Gameau, *That Sugar Film*, Documentary, Madman Entertainment and Goldwyn Films, 2015.
11. May, *Addiction & Grace*, 29.
12. C. S. Lewis, *The Problem of Pain* (New York: HarperOne, 1940), 74–75.

Chapter 3
1. C. S. Lewis, *The Problem of Pain* (New York: HarperOne, 1940), 24.
2. Gregory A. Boyd, *Satan and the Problem of Evil: Constructing a Trinitarian Warfare Theodicy* (Downers Grove, Illinois: InterVarsity Press, 2001), 182–183.
3. Jonathan Edwards and Reiner Smolinski, ed., "Sinners in the Hands of an Angry God: A Sermon Preached at Enfield, July 8th, 1741," Electronic Texts in

American Studies, Paper 54, http://digitalcommons.unl.edu/etas/54.

4. James Morgenstern quoted in Gregory A. Boyd, *God at War: The Bible & Spiritual Conflict* (Downers Grove, Illinois: InterVarsity Press, 1997), 147.

5. Boyd, *God at War*, 94.

6. Ibid., 152.

Chapter 4

1. C. S. Lewis, *The Lion, the Witch and the Wardrobe* (New York: HarperCollins, 1950), 168.

2. Gregory A. Boyd and Paul R. Eddy, *Across the Spectrum: Understanding Issues in Evangelical Theology* (Grand Rapids, MI: Baker Academic, 2002), 107.

3. Philip Yancey, *The Jesus I Never Knew* (Grand Rapids, MI: Zondervan, 1995), 37.

4. Vernard Eller, *The Most Revealing Book of the Bible: Making Sense Out of Revelation* (Grand Rapids, MI: William B Eerdmans, 1974), 77.

5. Ibid., 78–79.

6. Ibid., 176–177.

Chapter 5

1. C. S. Lewis, *The Problem of Pain* (New York: HarperOne, 1940), 70.

2. Gerald G. May, M.D., *Addiction & Grace: Love and Spirituality in the Healing of Addictions* (New York: HarperOne, 1988), 38.

3. Ibid., 105.

4. A. W. Tozer, *The Pursuit of God* (Lexington, KY: SoHo Books, 2010), 11.

5. Dietrich Bonhoeffer, *The Communion of Saints* (New York: Harper & Row, 1963), 71.

6. May, *Addiction & Grace*, 95.

7. Dallas Willard, *Renovation of the Heart: Putting on the Character of Christ* (Colorado Springs: NavPress, 2002), 68.

Chapter 6

1. "The Citarum River in Indonesia is So Polluted that You Can't Even See the Water," Strange Sounds, March 20, 2014, http://strangesounds.org/2014/03/the-citarum-river-in-indonesia-is-so-polluted-that-you-cant-even-see-the-water-photos-and-video.html

2. "These are the Dirtiest and Cleanest Rivers in the World," Global Citizen,

NOTES

https://www.globalcitizen.org/en/content/clean-dirty-rivers-water-polluted/

3. Gregory A. Boyd, *Seeing Is Believing: Experience Jesus through Imaginative Prayer* (Grand Rapids, MI: Baker Books, 2004), 91.

Chapter 7

1. Dallas Willard, *The Spirit of the Disciplines: Understanding How God Changes Lives* (New York: HarperOne, 1988), 91.

2. Ibid., 92.

3. Gerald G. May, M.D., *Addiction & Grace: Love and Spirituality in the Healing of Addictions* (New York: HarperOne, 1988), 85.

4. Ibid., 90.

Chapter 8

1. C. S. Lewis, *The Lion, the Witch and the Wardrobe* (New York: HarperCollins, 1950), 130–132.

Chapter 9

1. Gerald G. May, M.D., *Addiction & Grace: Love and Spirituality in the Healing of Addictions* (New York: HarperOne, 1988), 105, 141.

2. Ibid., 146–147.

3. Ibid., 141.

4. Ibid., 177.

5. Dallas Willard, *The Spirit of the Disciplines: Understanding How God Changes Lives* (New York: HarperOne, 1988), 158..

6. Alan D. Lieberson, "How long can a person survive without food?" Scientific American, https://www.scientificamerican.com/article/how-long-can-a-person-sur/

7. Sonya Shafer, *Laying Down the Rails for Yourself: Good Habits Are Not Just for Kids* (Lawrenceville, GA: Simply Charlotte Mason, 2016), 37.

Chapter 10

1. Gregory A. Boyd, *Seeing is Believing: Experience Jesus through Imaginative Prayer* (Grand Rapids, MI: Baker Books, 2004), 150.

2. Ibid., 115–116.

3. John Eldredge, *Free to Live: The Utter Relief of Holiness* (New York: Faith Words, 2013), 132.

4. Brother Lawrence, *The Practice of the Presence of God*, Edited by Whitaker House (New Kensington, PA: Whitaker House, 1982), 52.

Chapter 11

1. Janet and Geoff Benge, *Gladys Aylward: The Adventure of a Lifetime* (Seattle: YWAM, 1998), 198.

2. Dallas Willard, *Renovation of the Heart: Putting on the Character of Christ* (Colorado Springs: NavPress, 2002), 84.

3. Melissa and Dallas Hartwig, *Whole 30: The 30-Day Guide to Total Health and Food Freedom* (New York: Houghton Mifflin Harcourt), 5.

4. Dallas Willard, *The Spirit of the Disciplines: Understanding How God Changes Lives* (New York: HarperOne, 1988), 172.

5. Gerald G. May, M.D., *Addiction & Grace: Love and Spirituality in the Healing of Addictions* (New York: HarperOne, 1988), 106.

Chapter 12

1. A. W. Tozer, *The Pursuit of God* (Lexington, KY: SoHo Books, 2010), 5.

www.ingramcontent.com/pod-product-compliance
Lightning Source LLC
LaVergne TN
LVHW090115080426
835507LV00040B/893